DAILY MEDITATIONS

« Each precious stone is a reflection of the divine world, a reminder of the limpid purity and perfection of heaven. »

Omraam Mikhaël Aïvanhov

Cover illustration: Topaz

OMRAAM MIKHAËL AÏVANHOV

DAILY MEDITATIONS

Volume 9

PROSVETA

Prosveta S.A – B.P.12 – 83601 Fréjus CEDEX (France)

ISBN 2-85566-766-6

Every morning, before you do anything else, you must give yourself a few quiet moments of reflection so as to begin your day in peace and harmony, and unite yourself to the Creator by dedicating the new day to him through prayer and meditation.

It is the beginning that is all-important, for it is then, at the beginning, that new forces are set in motion and given direction. If we want to act wisely and well, we have to begin by casting some light on the situation. You do not look for something or start work in the dark; you start by lighting a lamp so that you can see what you are doing. And you can apply the same principle to every area in life: in order to know what to do and how to do it, you have to switch on the light—in other words, to concentrate and look into yourself. Without this light you will wander in all directions and knock on many different doors, and you will never achieve anything worth while.

Our days follow the direction that we give to our first thoughts in the morning, for, depending on whether we are mindful or not, we either clear the way ahead or litter it with all kinds of useless and even dangerous debris. Disciples of initiatic science know how to begin the day so that it may be fruitful and rich in God's grace, and so that they may share that grace with those around them. They understand how important it is to begin the day with one fundamental thought around which all the other thoughts of the day may revolve.

If you keep your sights fixed on a definite goal, a clear orientation, an ideal, all your activities will gradually organize themselves and fall into line in such a way as to contribute to the realization of that ideal. Even the negative or alien thoughts or feelings that attempt to infiltrate you will be deflected and put at the service of the divine world. Yes, even they will be forced to follow the direction you have chosen. In this way, thanks to the fundamental thought that you place in your head and your heart first thing in the morning, your whole day will be recorded in the book of life.

And, since everything we do is recorded, once you have lived one glorious day, one day of eternal life, not only will that day be recorded, not only will it never die, but it will endeavour to get the days that follow to imitate it. Try to live just one day as well as you possibly can, therefore, and it will influence all your days: it will persuade them to listen to its testimony and follow its example, so as to be well balanced, orderly, and harmonious.

Omraam Mikhaël Aïvanhov

People say such complicated things about spirituality, but actually it is all so simple: just choose an elevated thought or feeling, and concentrate on this day after day with all your love and attention, working away at it as if you are digging out a little inner furrow. Once this furrow has been formed, all your spiritual work will flow more easily. But please take this seriously. I have revealed so many truths to you, and supplied so many methods for your use, and now the decision is yours: make full use of them so they become part of you, and produce results. This is what 'living a spiritual life' means. Spirituality is not just an imaginary, airy-fairy subject, providing comfort and a topic for conversation. The word 'spirit', which is the root of the word 'spiritual', must not be made into an excuse for weird and wonderful fantasies. 'Life' is the key word in the expression 'spiritual life'. Yes, 'living' means investing divine realities with firm substance and form, integrating them solidly and unshakeably into yourself. Work like an engraver etching a fine design in matter – the matter of your own being. This design is a truth, or a word such as 'love', 'light', 'peace' or 'goodness'. Such words are precious gems which will, one day, become brilliantly encrusted in you.

There is only one true union possible for us human beings: the inner fusion with the divine principle that dwells within each one of us. The moment we achieve this contact a spark is discharged, our whole being suddenly begins vibrating in unison with divine immensity, and melts into this immensity. This union transforms our entire existence. Work towards experiencing this fusion at least once in a lifetime, for it will live on as a droplet of light within you, opening up your consciousness to your divine origin – your true self. You must continue to sustain this union until you achieve the perfection of all knowledge, and all powers. When you reach this point your true work begins: you have crossed to another shore, and are setting out on the path of perfection, but the journey ahead is long. You have captured one droplet of light, and thanks to this light you can drink from – and rejoice in – the ocean of light. But be aware that you are not yet united with the whole: you must continue to advance until you become one with the entire ocean of divine light. Then, truly, you will be reunited with your divine self.

The book of Genesis tells the story of Jacob's ladder, of how he fell asleep with his head upon a stone, and how, while he slept, he saw angels ascending and descending a ladder linking earth with heaven. This is how the hierarchy of the cosmos, which cabbalists know as the Tree of Life, was revealed to him.

Earth and heaven are not separate: a whole circulation of exchanges takes place between them. Clairvoyants may see beings descending to work on human beings, animals, plants and stones. Some of these beings may return immediately, whereas others stay longer to continue their work. Nowadays, few people believe in the existence of these creatures and their work; but one day all humankind will become conscious of this continuous movement between earth and heaven, between the earth and the sun, even to the limits of the universe, and on into infinite space.

Before we are born we exist in the obscurity of night, and everything is prepared in this darkness for our eventual birth. Every human organ – lungs, heart, brain etc. – is constructed within the obscurity of the mother's womb. If conditions influencing this formation are not good, the whole future life will be jeopardized, because day – earthly life, depends upon the previous night – gestation.

Every manifestation is like a coloured thread unwinding from a multicoloured ball. We see these threads unrolling and separating from the ball – but, first, they must have been wound on to that ball. So you see, if we have never used wisdom to prepare our thoughts, we cannot hope to draw wisdom out of our heads. Whatever we would like to manifest must be prepared a long time ahead. Do not be deluded: if we have not worked for a long time in the night, in the invisible world, nothing can be achieved in daylight, in the visible world.

The act of breathing, like eating, puts us in contact with universal life. But we must be fully aware, and at the same time work with our thoughts, in order to experience the wealth and completeness of this connection.

Try this exercise: expel air, imagining you are stretching out to the limits of the universe. Then, breathing in, turn back to yourself, towards your ego, the imperceptible point that is at the centre of an infinite circle – the circle of infinity. Again, expand yourself, again bring yourself back to that tiny point ... Thus you discover the movement of flux and reflux which is the key to all universal rhythms. Try to make this a conscious inner movement, and you will become part of cosmic harmony. There will be an intercourse between yourself and the universe, because when you inhale you receive elements from space and, in exchange, when you exhale you project something from your heart and soul. When we know how to harmonize ourselves with the respiration of the cosmos, then we enter divine consciousness.

Initiatic science teaches that the entity we call 'God' is both masculine and feminine, both the heavenly Father and the divine Mother. We are created in the image of God so we, too, are likewise polarized, and possess both masculine and feminine attributes inside ourselves. Of course, we have to leave our heavenly Father and Mother when we incarnate. We are obliged to leave our heavenly parents, but we must not cut the link with them. They do not cast us off without support as they have provided the means to keep in touch: the soul – feminine, and the spirit – masculine. Yes, but the soul and the spirit are not inert material, like a cord or a chain, they are living entities. In order to stay linked with the heavenly Father and the divine Mother we must work with wisdom – the masculine principle, and love – the feminine principle, because all other attributes of God flow from the basis of these two principles. Just as only opposite poles can attract, so the soul must work with wisdom to link with the heavenly Father, and the spirit must work with love to link with the divine Mother. Therefore, our spirit must keep in contact with the Mother by means of love, and our soul must link with the Father through wisdom.

Every living being is inextricably linked, however diverse their natural habitat may be. Whether or not we are conscious of this fact, we are linked with every being inferior to us, as we are with all those who are superior. There is a living hierarchy in nature, and it is this hierarchy, this link uniting us with all the higher beings, which gives us the potential to rise higher. However, remember that we are also powerfully attached to all the beings which exist below us – animals, plants and stones.

If our thoughts, feelings and actions are honest and pure, we are able to receive all the beneficial forces pouring down from heaven through this unbroken chain of living beings. This divine outpouring does not stop when it reaches us – it flows through us, streaming through the whole chain to the lower animal, vegetable and mineral realms. This is how, when we live in a state of harmony, we can exert a valuable influence everywhere, not only on everybody around us, but also on our brothers and sisters – the animals, plants and stones.

It is important to learn to work with the Sephirotic Tree, but if we wish to obtain great enlightenment we must embark on this knowledge with much humility. It is not enough to scan the diagram of this tree once or twice, learning the names so as to converse intelligently on the subject. To be the basis of true spiritual work, the Sephirotic Tree must become a permanent subject of meditation. Try to assimilate the ideas slowly, and digest them. Yes, digest them... It may be surprising that I use words normally applied to nutrition; I do so precisely because meditation on the Sephirotic Tree *is* a form of nutrition. We eat every day to keep ourselves healthy. Every day we eat different foods, choosing from amongst a great number of possible nutriments. The principle is the same when we contemplate the Sephirotic Tree: we discover an immense variety of 'food', because it is a reflection of the whole universe, containing not only religion, philosophy and true morality, but also every science and art form. So it is up to us to learn to choose our daily nourishment from this rich source.

January 11

Economics is the science of prediction. In order to be a good economist we need to look at long-term results, and not be seduced by solutions that appear good on a short-term time scale. It is very difficult to turn back once we have embarked on an enterprise that later proves hazardous – how often this happens!

'But what are we to do, since most of us have no influence in government affairs?' you remark. Of course, I do not intend you to intervene personally, rather understand that economics is not confined to economists: it is also the concern of each one of us. In our capacity as human beings, as cells in a living organism, we can act, but in order to do so we must develop our awareness and sense of responsibility. If we are not fully conscious, we participate in an economy which, instead of bringing prosperity, causes the ruination of many countries.

The luminous spirits of the invisible world ceaselessly exchange communications of love: they meet in space, exchange greetings, penetrate each other with rays of light, and then continue on their way. It is not necessary to possess a physical body in order to make exchanges – you also make thousands of exchanges of a non-physical nature with the beings around you. You don't kiss everybody, nor do you enfold everybody in your arms, but you constantly have encounters which nourish and make you happy. Why not increase the quantity and quality of these exchanges? Love – as understood by the majority of people – is really only slavery. In fact, insufficient words exist to describe the imperfections of such a love: it is greedy, selfish, possessive, jealous and cruel. You argue that your body is only human and therefore you cannot behave like an angel. However, know that it is not your physical body, but lack of control in your mind and emotions, that most hinders any spiritual expression of love. A human body is not what prevents us from the spiritual concept of love, for our soul and spirit are just as real as our physical body, and can intercommunicate with every other soul and spirit throughout the universe.

All those who try to enter the spiritual world without first working to prepare themselves, are confronted by a terrible being known to initiatic science as the Guardian of the Threshold. Really, this being is not outside them, it is within, a formation of the accumulation of all their inferior inclinations – desires, sensuality, agressivity, and so on, and he bars the way, because such people have no right to enter the spiritual world. Each of us must one day meet and confront the Guardian of the Threshold. He exists in Yesod, the ninth sephiroth. His frightful appearance threatens any adept presumptuous enough to venture into spiritual realms without the adequate preparation of work on purity, self-mastery, and courage. Only a disciple who has managed to dominate all his inferior instincts, and is armed with the necessary knowledge, can vanquish the Guardian of the Threshold. One look is all that is necessary – 'Go away!' – and this terrible being disappears, leaving the path ahead clear.

2 is the number of initiation. The most profound, complex and dangerous questions are contained within the 2, because this number holds the key to all division and separation. But division may also produce a third factor – the germination of a seed is an obvious example. If a grain of wheat is to germinate, it must divide. Before sprouting, the seed is *1*, when sown, it becomes 2. Then follows *3*: the embryo pushes out, drawing nourishment from the two halves of the seed. The two principles feed the third element, so it can grow. Therefore, within the seed there is first of all division, then fermentation, and then the seed itself begins to disappear, and dies. This death plays its part not only in nature, but also in our inner life. Thanks to this death, we awaken to a new life. Jesus said, '... unless a grain of wheat falls into the earth and dies, it remains just a single grain; but if it dies, it bears much fruit.'

January 15

Each one of us must know when to show leniency and when to show severity – the whole of life and society is based on the balance between these two extremes. If we are always strict, or always indulgent, what happens? Strength and gentleness are permanently opposite qualities, of course, and one cannot expect them to be otherwise. Both are necessary in life and in nature, just as they are, and our work is to know how to make use of them. When you need to act with severity, awaken tolerance in your heart, so you do not become hard and unjust. Do the opposite when you want to show kindness: keep an element of severity so that your kindness is not taken as a sign of weakness, or that you will tolerate bad behaviour. Yes, a correct balance always has to be found, and that is difficult.

The physical body is difficult to transform because its matter is opaque, resistant, and rebellious. But there are other areas made of subtler matter – our feelings and thoughts – and these are easier to work with, enhance, and make more beautiful. So, begin working on these areas, and the physical body will follow, much more slowly, of course, but that does not matter. What is important is the knowledge that we can improve our whole state through the quality of our thoughts and feelings. Certainly this work will not produce immediate and spectacular physical changes, but little by little our inner work will transform our bodies, too.

Everything in our homes, the walls and every object, is impregnated with our emanations. Our very presence works magic, spreading a covering over everything around us which acts as a good, or bad, conductor of divine influences. If we constantly give out negative feelings, words and thoughts, the objects around us act as magnets, attracting all that is dark and toxic in the universe. The opposite is also true. If we harbour thoughts and feelings of wisdom and love, and pronounce life-giving words, we spread good fluids on all the objects around us, so they become conductors of light, joy and health.

So, when you are at home, learn to touch every object with love, blessing them, asking the divine Spirit to visit them. Say: 'Spirit of light, purity, and truth, I consecrate these objects for your use, may they become a receptacle for you.' And the divine Spirit will come to dwell in your home.

January 19

To assess the qualities of people, an initiate uses certain criteria which are not in general use. Appraisal of others is normally based on social position, wealth, academic status, or behaviour patterns, and responsibility or privileges are granted according to exterior qualities. That is why so many mistakes are made, because the essential element – character – has not been taken into account. An initiate does the opposite, evaluating character alone. He is not at all impressed by exterior acquisitions, too easily gained – a few years, or months, are all that is needed to acquire savoir-faire, academic status, or even wealth. But centuries and millenniums are necessary to obtain and develop unselfishness, loyalty, goodness, generosity, and courage. These are the only qualities an initiate takes into consideration.

Books on the occult provide plenty of information on how to become clairvoyant, such as gazing into a crystal or magic mirror, use of plants, hypnosis, and so on. But all these methods are unwholesome or dangerous, and it is strongly advisable not to try to develop clairvoyance without first achieving purity. Of course, it is possible to become clairvoyant without first purifying ourselves, because it is not such a difficult faculty to develop. The problem is that if we are not pure it is not the divine world we shall see, rather the shadowy entities that lurk around ourselves and others. We shall see wickedness, betrayal and lies. We shall see impending disasters. In other words, what we see depends on the level of our evolution: we can only see a world that corresponds to this level, or somewhat further.

Jesus said: 'Blessed are the pure in heart, for they shall see God.' The best way to obtain true clairvoyance – the sight of the divine world, is to develop within ourselves purity and spiritual love.

Each word carries a certain resonance or vibration, which gives it the power to act either constructively or destructively. Most people are not aware of this fact, which is why their words alone cause so much damage and misery. Every word pronounced arouses feelings. That is why, if we speak with constructive and inspiring words, their corresponding feelings are very soon aroused. When an actor sets foot on the stage he cannot immediately experience the emotions his role requires him to express. But as soon as he begins to speak, the very words he utters make him experience these emotions with increasing intensity, and he is then able to communicate these emotions to the audience. The words themselves release energies, and these energies act upon the public. On reflection, it is clear that we must be extremely careful about our words, and watch that we do not speak carelessly, using negative words which create unhappiness and devastation.

Even when they claim to have opted for a spiritual way of life, some people still occupy their minds too much with material concerns: money, social position, fame, power, and so forth. That is why they cannot understand the truths of an initiatic teaching, and why they do not progress. Obviously, because we live on earth, we cannot possibly avoid material responsibilities. However, there are ways of reconciling our preoccupations with the life of the spirit: the first thing we must settle, before anything else, is the question of our goal and the means by which we achieve this goal. Instead of making money, power, and fame our objective, and using the methods of initiatic science to achieve these objectives, we must do the opposite. Our ideal must be the divine life, and everything we possess must be used for this purpose. Then we will achieve real progress.

We wish to instruct or heal others, but before making any attempt to do so, it is wise to study, because without proper training it is too easy to make mistakes. Sometimes it is essential to study conventional sciences – medicine, for example. There are people who have acquired a degree of magnetism because of their immense love of their fellow human beings, and because they have worked on certain virtues, and they can use this power with beneficial effect on the physical body – of this there is no doubt. Such people, however, are rare. If you wish to cure people you must start by studying, otherwise there is a danger you will make matters worse. Conventional medical practice is not ideal, because very often only the physical body is examined, and all that lies over and above the physical state is ignored; but the groundwork of knowledge it offers is essential. Then, if you want to continue further and decide to concentrate your research on more subtle, spiritual, aspects of healing, this is commendable. But know that, in order to care for people, preliminary study is always essential.

January 25

You have an apple or a pear, or some such fruit. This fruit has already been picked, and if you examined it through scientific instruments you would see that it differs from a similar fruit still attached to its tree. On the tree living forces flow through this fruit, and it is supplied with sap elaborated by the whole universe. The moment the fruit is picked, it no longer receives these energies.

The same applies to human beings: people must be studied while still linked to the Cosmic Tree, because there they are alive, gifted and radiant. That is why science, which likes to study people when they are, as it were, cut off from the Tree of Life, cannot really know what human life is: they only study corpses. You could say: 'Yes, but at least we can dissect a corpse and see how it is made. We can't do that to a living body.' Well, this just proves that other means of studying the human body while it is whole and alive need to be found, without cutting it into pieces. And these means do exist. When we have them at our disposal, we will discover all the subtle currents circulating through us, linking us to the whole universe.

January 27

The phenomena of transformation of movement into heat and light and, conversely, the transformation of light into heat and movement, are very well known and widely used in physics. The only people who have no understanding of these facts are indolent spiritualists, who are happy merely to meditate, study and reflect, without bothering to transform this light into heat – feelings – and movement – action. If you were to ask some of them to work physically they would be scandalized. How could anyone ask them to do something so beneath them? Well, that is where they go wrong. Physical work is essential for the evolution of each one of us. So, even if nobody forces us, we must compel ourselves to find some physical tasks, otherwise our bodies will suffer, and even our minds and emotions will be affected. If only you understood the benefits of physical activity, which enlightens our awareness and helps us advance spiritually as well, you would do everything in your power to make sure that you always have something to clean, wash, plant, sew or repair.

January 28

Religion and moral doctrine teach renunciation and sacrifice, but the meaning of these concepts has not yet been truly understood. Renunciation is not privation. To renounce means to move up from one place to another, accomplishing on a higher plane what we were accustomed to do on a lower plane. For example, instead of drinking water from swamps swarming with bacteria – this is symbolic – we must get into the habit of drinking the water from a crystal-clear spring. If we do not drink, we die. If someone says: 'I'm never going to drink again!' he will dehydrate, and die. It is the water from sewers that we must not drink. We need to drink, but we must drink celestial water.

In every area of life, equilibrium depends on the existence of the two complementary forces, masculine and feminine. This is why the current trend for men and women to behave identically, to dress alike, and follow the same occupations, is rather disturbing.

What will happen to our psychological state if women end up fighting wars, while men nurse babies? When all polarity disappears, so does procreation. If these two poles, these two electrodes, are not totally different, then they can no longer produce any sparks, any life. It is perfectly normal for women to wish for the same freedom as men, and to show just as much initiative, but they can achieve all this without imitating men, or trying to replace them, or even getting rid of them. Freedom, daring, and a spirit of initiative are all qualities which women can develop, and that is good if, at the same time, they also augment and enhance their quintessential femininity.

January 30

It is dangerous to attempt to enter the spiritual world without first purifying ourselves, because in that realm much is beyond the capacity of the intellect: to a much greater extent it encompasses the totality of the human being and our most intimate, innermost motivating forces, and that is why we need to be extremely careful. To work with the soul and the spirit is to work with the two fundamental principles of creation, and therefore to be in touch with the most powerful entities and currents in the universe. If the inner paths are blocked, and if these currents encounter impurities, they burn everything in their path. This is a terrible fire, which can produce the very worst mental, emotional, and even physical disturbances – unbridled sensuality and mental unbalance – and physiological upsets of the heart and brain. Those who aspire to regions of light and divine love must be inspired by the highest ideal, by the sole desire to become perfect, and to serve the will of God.

January 31

To understand how psychic energies circulate and work in human beings, we have to observe how they circulate and work in nature. Look at a tree: the higher its trunk and branches, the deeper its roots descend into the ground. This system of compensation exists on every plane, whether physical, mental, emotional, or spiritual. So the higher our consciousness rises, the deeper we must descend into our subconscious.

Those who decide to embrace the life of the spirit make a great mistake if they disregard the reality of the obscure world inside themselves. They imagine that just wanting to work for the light, to be wise, just and unselfish, is enough to guarantee that they achieve these qualities. Sadly, it is not so. Every level of consciousness attained corresponds to certain currents, energies, and entities, and a spiritual person must watch carefully to maintain a correct balance between these two worlds.

Fair exchange is the basis of all social life, and is a maxim which can be resumed very simply: give and take. Obviously, everyone knows about fair and equitable exchange in the material world, but there is much more to it, because the law of exchange applies to all other levels of existence. You may say: 'I am an honest and upright citizen, I pay my dues, I remunerate my employees very decently, and would never dream of cheating or deceiving my clients.' This may be so, but do you treat your parents, spouse and children in the same way? It is much easier to be honest and just in the material world than it is where the mind and emotions are involved. Some people go to great lengths to show their honesty and even-handedness, in order to conceal dishonest dealings in their personal relationships: maybe their relatives and friends can be easily taken in – although they are not always fooled – but divine justice can never be duped. Divine justice and human justice hold very different views on the true meaning of giving and taking.

Whenever we experience one thing, in every area of life, it is not long before we encounter its opposite. Even within ourselves there is a continuous succession of opposing states – sleeping and waking, work and rest, health and illness, weakness and strength, sadness and joy – all these different states and conflicting energies are necessary, only we must be alert and remember that after happiness we must expect sadness, and after hope, discouragement, and vice versa.

Have you experienced a moment of great happiness? Then you must expect to be faced with something unpleasant, caused either by an outside event, or because of people around you, or even – if you do not know how to cherish this state of joy – by yourself. Yes, bear this in mind always, because if you are careless you will be caught off your guard. Do not be lulled into inattention after moments of great joy. You must be on your guard, for the other side is always there waiting to reveal itself, and if you are taken by surprise you could lose all the benefit you have already gained from such joy. This is a law. Everything is linked, and a movement in one area always triggers another movement in the opposing area.

Suppose you want to teach yourself the violin. You start by buying a violin and books of exercises, and begin playing. At first you play for one or two hours each day, but very soon enthusiasm flags, and you give up. Later you begin practising again, and again you give up. Things continue this way, alternating between activity and apathy, according to your mood. On the other hand, suppose you find a violin teacher: you would practise regularly, busily preparing for the next lesson and, of course, your teacher would always be at hand to correct faults and give encouragement. For the same reason, a master is an indispensable help in your spiritual work, as his presence encourages you to persevere in your efforts. 'But a spiritual master is the last person I need – extra effort is not my idea of fun!' you may say. Naturally, you are free to do as you please, but if you do not allow a master to instruct you, the only alternative is to accept lessons from life itself. And you can be perfectly sure of one thing: life, as a teacher, can be awesome and relentless.

Why do you sometimes hesitate before proffering kindness and generosity? Perhaps this is because you do not expect any thanks or recognition. You reckon that people are often ungrateful, even unkind, so you feel disinclined to make efforts on their behalf. Well, this is a very pernicious philosophy which could paralyse all your best intentions. Perhaps one of your good deeds passed unnoticed, or was even used against you. Please understand, once and for all, that you can never expect anything from other people. Therefore expect nothing, except from Him who is all-seeing and all-knowing, for He alone will appreciate your good and generous actions, and it is from Him that your reward will come. It may come in a different and totally unexpected form. Perhaps you will be granted better health, and more strength, wisdom and happiness: these, surely, are the best rewards of all.

A link exists between knowledge and our inner freedom. Because we tend to be bound up in preoccupations and worries, we are not free to ponder the essential truths which could help us find our way through life. Some think freedom is the most precious of all possessions, and they are ready to fight each other for it: but of course this is a different freedom, not the inner freedom which offers the means to discover and understand essential truths. These people fill their days with activities which monopolize their minds, enslaving and blinding them. They are like a man who walks through the most beautiful garden or glorious countryside, but he is so weighed down by troubles and worry he remains oblivious to all the wonders of heaven and earth around him, and in him. But unless he is free with an inner freedom, he sees nothing.

When you switch on your radio or television you can select the programme of your choice – music, a play, or the news. In the same way you can, inwardly, choose the programme you wish to listen to. But if you do not know how to find the right station, instead of sublime heavenly music you will receive nothing but infernal uproar and din.

If this happens, hurry to change your 'wavelength' as quickly as possible, using your imagination and thoughts to select another programme. And remember that your prayers are like very short high frequency waves: they are the best way to find the right programme, and connect with heaven.

Every human being needs to create. But unless we have developed faculties that allow contact with higher regions, our works will be mere copies or reproductions, and not true creations. Exactly the same phenomenon occurs when fathers and mothers reproduce their own weaknesses and short-comings in their children. They call it creation, but in fact it is only reproduction.

The Sephirotic Tree[1] is a graphic description of the different regions of the universe. It also represents every area of the human psyche, and helps us understand the path we have to follow to attain the invisible world. From the bottom, Malkouth is the first sephira – representing the physical plane, the earth. From Malkouth we leave the physical plane to enter the psychic plane – Yesod, the region of the moon. Yesod marks the beginning of all psychic life, and is a degree more advanced than Malkouth. We reach the first stage of psychic life on the lower level of Yesod, which the light of Tiphareth – the sun – has not yet been able to penetrate. This is a region of mists and vague indeterminate forms, and we must pass through this region very quickly and go higher, to the world of light and reason – the world of the spirit. Here, our real work begins.

---

1 See note and diagram, page 368

The whole subject of spirit and matter is limitless, encompassing many aspects: spirit and matter are also the masculine and feminine principles – positive and negative, emissive and receptive, heaven and earth. Nothing is more important than these two principles. But their place and role must be well understood, so one principle is not favoured at the expense of the other.

People always have a tendency to go to extremes: either they focus only on the spirit and neglect matter, or they focus on matter to the exclusion of the spirit. This is all too evident today: people tend to concentrate all their attention on material concerns, entirely neglecting the spiritual content. So matter remains as it is, crude and lifeless.

Why are some men and women so vibrant and expressive? Because the matter of their bodies is given life by the spirit within. How true this is! Somebody dies and the spirit leaves his body, so what more can be done, other than bury the remains? The spirit activates everything through the medium of matter. Matter is nothing without spirit; yet, without matter, the spirit is powerless.

If we have not taken proper control of our life, and if all the cells of our being are not synchronized with divine vibrations, we are at the mercy of the blind forces of nature. Cosmic laws cannot be contravened with impunity: whoever opposes cosmic intelligence will sooner or later disintegrate and disappear. You may think cosmic intelligence very cruel to destroy the creatures opposed to it. No, cosmic intelligence has nothing to do with human punishment – it never wants to destroy. But if we clash with cosmic order, through ignorance or ill will, the forces ranged against us are so powerful that we are demolished – quite naturally. If some poor idiot wants to confront a whole army, obviously he will be overwhelmed in a trice. When a bird keeps colliding with a window it ends up killing itself; but the window is not to blame. People behave like this bird: they rebel against divine laws, against the splendour of the universe, oblivious that they must pay the price for foolishness. They court danger, and pay the ultimate price: but it is not God who has destroyed them – they have destroyed themselves.

We are not accustomed to considering the profound meaning of every gesture, so we tend to make gestures automatically, from force of habit. You meet somebody for a talk, a meal or a business discussion, you begin by shaking hands, and this creates a bond. One hand represents the masculine, emissive principle, and the other the feminine, or receptive principle. If there is conscious thought behind this handshake, and if each hand fulfils its intended role, a positive state of harmony is formed. When two people shake hands they want to understand each other, and make progress together – but this will be achieved only if one of the hands possesses positive energy and the other, negative energy. The joining of two active and positive hands produces conflict, whereas two passive and negative hands shaken together results in inertia and ineffective results. The act of shaking hands always implies a wish to participate in some organized activity: it says, 'I would like to have dealings with you and see if we can collaborate.' Yes, before making any association, pay attention to this language of the hands, otherwise there could be many quarrels and much disillusion.

Suppose you own a field and sow it with good and bad seed simultaneously, both grow together, because the earth nurtures all seeds. You cannot tell the earth it is stupid, that it should stifle the weeds and only allow the good seeds to thrive. The earth will reply: 'I don't understand. I nurture and protect all seeds. So far as I'm concerned they are all good, even the bad ones are good.' If you project good thoughts, the harvest will be wonderful; but if you give out unworthy thoughts, nature will nourish and fortify these also, because the bad has just as much right to grow as the good, until it is ready for harvesting. However, when all has been harvested, the owner of the field will order the weeds to be burned and the good grain gathered into his barns. This is exactly what Jesus taught in the parable of the tares. He knew that evil has as much right to grow as good, but it is our responsibility not to sow the bad.

Many people think of spirituality as a kind of empty space into which they would have to throw themselves if they lead a spiritual life, and they are naturally fearful of committing themselves. Of course, jumping into a void is dangerous unless we have grown wings. But if we are inspired by a real desire to serve the spirit we can safely launch ourselves out into space with no fear of falling: our wings will unfold and we shall fly. If we remain rooted to the ground, never rising to the heights, we would not necessarily be safe – in fact the reverse is true – we would still be vulnerable to falling headlong. But if people choose to follow a spiritual path, and then have bad experiences, it is because their motivation is not pure, disinterested, and truly spiritual.

In order to understand the wealth of meaning contained in the number Ten, one must study both the One and the Zero separately. This study reveals that each digit has its own particular nature, its own particular function, and that they have specific work together. To understand this work, we have to realize that they are not simply placed side by side, but that the One penetrates the Zero in order to give it life and set it in motion. This notion is also expressed by the symbol of the dot in the centre of a circle ⊙.

Genesis begins with these words: 'In the beginning God created the heavens and the earth, and the earth was a formless void; and darkness covered the face of the deep, and a wind from God swept over the face of the waters.' The wind, or spirit, of God is the masculine principle, which hovers over matter – symbolized by the waters – in order to fertilize it. Water is the circle, the O, and the Spirit of God is the dot, the One. Unless it is animated by the Spirit, matter remains 'tohu va-bohu': formless and void. But when matter is overshadowed and fashioned by the spirit, all the potential it contains begins to manifest, and it becomes a universe, with suns, constellations and nebulae. Our universe therefore represents the Ten: matter, Zero, which has already been given life, fashioned, and organised by the One, the Spirit.

When we go out, walk in the streets, look at the shops, take a stroll in gardens or countryside, we are following the instinct to make exchanges with people and nature, because life depends on this intercourse. You wonder about the ascetics and hermits who have hidden from the world in caves and desert retreats, deliberately fleeing from all such communication? Yes, they have eschewed some exchanges in order to relate in a different way, opening their souls and spirits to more subtle, spiritual communication. As soon as we shut ourselves off from one influence, we automatically open to another. If we do not wish to see or hear on the physical plane, another inner vision and hearing will manifest, so we shall be able to capture other, new and subtle ideas. Exchanges are the quintessence of life: when we learn how to relate on the spiritual plane, we shall obtain knowledge of the true science of all life.

Observe yourselves, and you will realize that your emotional life is largely made up of a subtle interchange, or communication, of thoughts and feelings, which feeds and enriches you. You leave home in the morning, you meet friends you like or admire, you greet them and they return your greeting, and you all feel happy. These gestures of greeting are made through the intermediary of your feelings and thoughts, your soul and spirit. Even if you do not meet in the flesh people for whom you feel love and admiration, you can always hear on the radio, or see on television, people who do inspire such feelings. You may also be inspired and filled with wonder by reading, listening to beautiful music, or contemplating works of art. These experiences are all interchanges with other beings. Through their masterpieces artists give us something, and we give something in exchange, in the form of admiration and love. 'But many of them are dead!' you say. Physically that may be so, but the soul and spirit which created these masterpieces is immortal, always at hand to nourish and enrich our own souls and spirits.

Who or what is God? Many are the philosophers, theologians and mystics who have tried to answer this question, but none has really succeeded, because God cannot be explained in words. Only when we lose ourselves in God and become one with Him, can we know who He is. But even then, this knowledge will be ours alone. It is not possible to explain it to others.

The entity or being we call 'God' is both masculine and feminine, as I have already explained. When we speak of the cosmic spirit and the universal soul we are speaking about God as a single, unique being who is polarized. Although we can neither describe nor even conceive of such a being, we can draw closer to it. Through meditation and prayer our spirit enters into communion with the universal soul, and our soul with the cosmic spirit. In this way we achieve perfect fusion.

Our place in this universe is not as simple as that of a stone, plant or animal. Because we have the capacity to think our role is quite different: our work is to contribute towards building a collective life. If we work only for ourselves, nothing worthwhile will result. 'But if I work for my own good, I am better off!' No, this is not true, because the selfish, isolated 'self' you are working for is an abyss which swallows up without trace everything it can get. This is no way to waste your life. Selfish egocentrics are oblivious of the benefits they would enjoy if they worked for the good of the collectivity.

However, please understand what I mean by the word 'collectivity': this 'collectivity' is not confined to the human race, it encompasses the whole universe, all the beings who live there, and even God Himself. This collectivity, this immensity for whom you work is like a bank, and one day everything you paid in will return to you – with interest.

Genesis: says: 'In the beginning God created the heavens and the earth.' Heaven and earth, and the relationship existing between them, are symbols which need interpretation. Heaven and earth represent the two principles – masculine and feminine – emissive and receptive. These principles unite, and from this union children are born. Everything on earth is a product of the union of these two principles, the union of heaven and earth. If earth cuts this link with heaven, earth cuts all link with life, and if it no longer receives divine energy, it turns into an arid desert. Heaven and earth – the masculine and feminine principles – are realities in the sublime realms on high: all the intervening regions and domains, right down to the physical plane, mirror these two principles – heaven and earth, masculine and feminine. Wherever we look we see nothing but the union of these two principles.

Suppose for a moment that you have two identical tuning forks: if you make one vibrate, the other, from a distance, will begin to vibrate also. This phenomenon is known as resonance. It is common knowledge, but not everyone takes the time to reflect that the same phenomenon happens between human beings: if we tune our physical and psychic body to the vibrations of the universe we resonate with heavenly energies, receiving help and comfort. Yes, this is a way of communicating: when we speak, we are listened to, and help is sent. It is even possible, in this way, to tap into energies in space, and benefit from them. Now you understand the great importance of striving to surpass ourselves, of making our subtlest and most sensitive inner strings vibrate, so they resonate with their corresponding energies, entities, and regions: these will then reply.

Everything in the universe exists also in man, everything from stones and plants to the archangels and God Himself. This is why the universe is called the macrocosm – the big world, and man, the microcosm – the little world. Man is infinitely small and the universe infinitely large, but there are numerous corresponding features between these two worlds. All the organs of our physical body, as well as those of our mental, emotional, and spiritual bodies, have an affinity with various regions of the cosmos. Of course, the cosmos does not have organs identical to our own, but the quintessence of our organs corresponds exactly with those of the cosmos, and we are able to make contact with those energies and centres in space which, through the law of affinity, correspond to those same energies and centres within ourselves.

Every human being resembles a book, an autobiography, written by himself. But often this book contains nothing much more than scribbles and gibberish. So when two of these 'books' meet and, mutually besotted, they live in each others' pockets, night and day 'reading' each other, what good do you imagine comes from 'reading' of this kind?

People know many things, but they have not yet learned how to write their own 'book', and form a masterpiece of it. They have been taught how to work on many things outside themselves – sculpture, carving, writing, drawing, and so on – always external creations: but their inner lives are left neglected and unembellished.

However, once they have realised how important it is to write their own 'book', they will look forward to all sorts of wonderful 'reading' whenever they meet each other, and will wonder at the sublime beauty of the language and illustrations – the qualities, virtues and gifts – developed through their inner work.

Truth can be compared to a coin with love on one side and wisdom on the other. If you seek truth independently of love and wisdom, that is to say without the collaboration of the heart and intellect, you will never find it. But once you have love and wisdom you will find truth also, even if you are not looking for it. Truth is not autonomous. Truth exists only if we work together with the heart and intellect, at one and the same time. Nowadays so many different and contradictory truths exist in the world, because they are a reflection of the distortion of human hearts and minds. Someone claims: 'This is the truth!' Well, know this is not so: he is giving his own version of the truth, a reflection of his own heart and mind, which may be feeble and deformed or, on the other hand, very highly developed.

Study the profound meaning of day and night. Night is symbolically the domain of the invisible – the non-manifest, and day, all that is visible – the manifest. All that is manifest depends on the non-manifest, just as day depends on night.

It is during the 'night' – in the invisible – that events of the 'day' are prepared, because everything tangible is the result, the condensation, of something immaterial. This is how a clairvoyant foresees forthcoming events: they already exist in the invisible world. It takes time for these events to reach the physical plane, but they must eventually do so, because they have already been ordained on high. Watch how a snake moves: its tail always follows its head. The head represents the idea, the project, and the tail its tangible existence, the material formation of events already created and present in the invisible world.

We must not try to escape from suffering, rather we should draw on the strength in it to awaken our inner, sublime life. The precise role of suffering is this: to arouse qualities which would never have the chance to manifest under easier conditions. Whenever we have to suffer, physically, mentally or emotionally, thank heaven for the opportunity this suffering gives to do an important work on ourselves. Of course, I am not speaking about an intolerable physical suffering which obviously requires medical intervention; I am speaking in general terms, about the troubles and difficulties which beset us in everyday life. Instead of moaning and groaning, weeping, or raging against the Lord, you would do better trying to put your troubles to good use by working on your own development. Whatever you do, when you are having a bad time do not concentrate on your suffering, instead work to harmonize everything inside you, and become stronger. Do this, and your suffering will disappear, because the problem set for you by heaven has been solved.

We see how some people understand love, how they express this love, and the various methods they use to coerce their loved one, and it is clear that they may already be dabbling, albeit unconsciously, in black magic. The use of all possible means in an attempt to seduce somebody is nothing less than forcible violation, and nobody has the right to do so. But there are people who, swept away by infatuated emotions, are indifferent to whether the object of their love reciprocates their feelings, or not: they demand that their love be returned, at any price, and will resort to any methods, even witchcraft, to obtain their desires. I warn you: never do anything like this, for you will enter into relationship with diabolical energies and these, after you have made use of them, will sooner or later turn on you.

Thousands of theologians have depicted the devil as God's unconquerable enemy, so they conclude that God is not the all powerful Master governing the universe: since some entity is able to defy Him, logically that entity must be as powerful as Him, or even more powerful. Perhaps this thought never occurred to them. But it is so, and here is the proof: throughout Christendom, right through the middle ages and way beyond, whenever men or women showed exceptional faculties they were accused of making a pact with the devil to receive diabolic gifts. Unfortunately, the church contributed to the spread of this belief. Yes, the church is responsible for the position accorded the devil in Christianity. Prophesies, the healing of the sick, or divine inspiration were all presumed to be the work of the devil, and not of heaven. So it is not surprising that some people did, in fact, seek to make a pact with the devil: what would be the use of serving some incompetent God, since the church proclaimed that all knowledge and gifts were provided by His enemy – the devil? In a way, their reasoning is correct: but without the true initiatic knowledge of good and evil, we too could easily jump to absurd conclusions of this kind.

What is it that certain clairvoyants see, and how can these visions be explained? Think of it like this: the nature of a vision is exactly the same as that of a dream. It is merely a question of the degree of consciousness: whether it comes from a state of wakefulness, or sleep. Can we believe these visions? Yes, but only to the extent that those dreams, or visions, provide information about the dreamer or clairvoyant, and their level of evolution. Dreams and visions always have a meaning, but those who have not managed to free themselves from the lower astral plane will receive their visions and dreams from these shadowy regions. Obviously, they cannot be confident of receiving clear knowledge or precise answers to their questions. We can have confidence in the messages in our dreams and visions only when we have managed to elevate ourselves to the causal, buddhic, and atmic planes[1].

---

1 See note and diagram, pages 366-367

We leave beneficial, or malevolent, traces – rather like invisible fingerprints – everywhere we go and on whatever we touch. It is said that wherever some people tread, the grass grows no more. Of course, this idea is symbolic, but it is no exaggeration. Other beings have the opposite effect: they are so richly endowed with love and goodness they cover everything in their wake with traces so beneficial that all who follow in their footsteps feel enlightened, warmed and revived.

This is why we too, wherever we pass, should remember to say aloud a few words of blessing and good wishes, such as: 'May light shine on all who pass this way. Whoever they may be, they are all children of God, so let them work for peace and brotherhood!'

This may be the first time you have heard such a suggestion. But why wait to be prompted? Do you have to be told to send greetings and good wishes to your nearest and dearest? Of course not. You do it spontaneously, prompted by your affectionate feelings. Why not, then, spontaneously send greetings and wishes for the whole of creation?

All humankind, the solar system, and even the whole cosmos, must undergo events decreed since the beginning of time, and there is nothing we can do to change this. Imagine we are cruising on board a ship: there is a prearranged itinerary and scheduled ports of call which are, of course, impossible to alter, and there is no way we can leave this ship – unless we fall overboard. However, on board we can read, enjoy conversing with our fellow travellers, sleep in our cabins, or visit the bridge to scan the ocean. This metaphor of a ship illustrates the destiny of humankind: we are all on board a ship whose itinerary has been mapped out by the Lord himself, and there is absolutely nothing that anybody can do to change it. 'On board' – inwardly – we may do as we please, we can improve or demean ourselves, but our scheduled destination remains the same.

Whenever evil forces have been unleashed people have always come forward to speak out on behalf of justice and goodness: they would never have had such an exceptional opportunity to show their true measure if such events had never occurred. So, enemies and trials actually compel us to draw upon inner resources which would otherwise have remained hidden – unknown and undetected. Opposition makes it necessary to exert ourselves: our struggles to overcome obstructions oblige us to unearth and use our own hidden inner potential and, in this way, we become aware of our true value. This may be difficult – and so it is – but it is the only way we can surmount the obstacles on our path. So, instead of complaining and rebelling, thank God and say: 'Because of these difficulties I will become strong, and surpass myself.' Evil and affliction are a needle which goads us on to ever greater efforts.

On the surface you appear to be well behaved and reasonable – or, so it would seem. We all live by certain established rules and we all try to respect the laws of society. But the way in which innermost thoughts and feelings behave is quite another matter: mentally and emotionally they are capable of stealing, destroying, killing, and then you wonder why you are unhappy, weak, confused or ill. If only you would pause a moment and take a good, honest look at yourselves: it would be obvious that you had, at some time or another, entertained very negative thoughts and feelings, without realizing the devastation these thoughts and feelings cause. So, the responsibility for your present pitiful state rests on your shoulders alone, and you must accept that responsibility. Not only do you have to face the consequences of your words, gestures and actions, but you must realize that everything that happens deep down inside you leaves scars, because a whole chain of reactions has been stirred up and set in motion, with ineluctable results – whether good, or evil.

A speaker may be taken over by a powerful surge of psychic energy, mesmerizing his audience, but that does not mean that he is 'inspired' in any real sense. It is essential to know the origin of inspiration, and from whence it springs. This must be clearly understood: because somebody has the power to galvanize crowds and hold them under his spell does not mean that he is really inspired – in the sense that initiates understand inspiration. Politicians are often a case in point. There is no doubt about their rhetorical gifts, but often this is no more than an ability to express very mundane matters in a dramatic way. In fact they merely express very ordinary thoughts and feelings, but with great emphasis: the quality of what they say contains nothing admirable. True inspiration, on the other hand, implies exceptional quality and is infused with elements of great purity and subtlety. True inspiration is divine inspiration.

God sends us initiates, sages and great masters to enlighten us, and help us understand the existence of laws which must be obeyed. And because we have a tendency not to understand, God sends beings who stir our feelings by their suffering and sacrifice on our behalf. The first are sent to appeal to our intellect, and the second to touch our hearts. If, despite this, we fail to understand these lessons, He has no alternative but to resort to force, so He sends us violent thugs, tyrants and butchers who oppress and persecute us. Yes, all the terrible events in the world at this moment are a direct consequence of the fact that human beings have not wanted to understand the teaching of wisdom and love.

All of us are visited by spirits of light, or of darkness, for we supply sustenance for either light, or darkness. The spirits we attract are either divine or diabolical, according to how we live our lives and what ideals we aspire to. So we must set ourselves a considerable programme of work, fashioning our own matter to attract spirits of light and making ourselves a dwelling place for the Divinity. If we want the Spirit to descend into us we must dedicate ourselves to heaven, saying: 'O heavenly angels, archangels and divinities, servants of almighty God and the divine Mother, take me, and everything I possess, so that the Kingdom of God may come on earth and the Golden Age reign amongst all peoples.' Until we dedicate ourselves to heaven we remain uncommitted and ignorant of which master we serve. If this is so, we are of no use to anyone, least of all to ourselves.

On the Tree of Life music belongs in the sephira Chokmah, ruled by the Cherubim.[1] Chokmah is the realm of the Word, by which everything was created, and the Word is nothing other than music, the harmonious sounds and chords that fashioned cosmic matter. Sound models and forms matter, and this is how God used the Word to fashion formless matter, the 'tohu va bohu' in Genesis. He spoke upon this cosmic dust, and forms came into being. The Cherubim received the divine vibration of the Word, and this vibration was communicated to every other creature existing throughout space. When we sing the mystical songs of the Brotherhood as a choir, we too link with the order of Cherubim. This harmony works on us, resonating within every particle of our being, communicating its harmonious vibrations, and shaping us in the form of perfect beauty.

---

1 See note and diagram, page 368

Who controls human beings? Do you think it is we, ourselves – in the sense of our divine Self – who rules supreme? On the contrary: chaotic and obscure forces have supplanted the divine Self, relegating it to solitary confinement like a prisoner on a diet of a few crusts of bread and water. It suffers wretchedly, but is forced to submit to these dominant forces and satisfy their whims. We must see this for what it is: real anarchy – an inner anarchy that is far more serious and threatening than anything of a social or political kind. This is the type of anarchy which fills prisons, hospital wards and mental asylums. So it is up to each one of us to be wary and watchful, to allow divine authority – the sovereignty of the divine Principle – to reign over us again.

We descended from heavenly regions through a process known as involution. The further we descend into matter the further we distance ourselves from primordial fire, assuming increasingly denser bodies until, eventually, we enter the physical body. It is as if we are dressing for the cold of winter: wrapping ourselves in layers of clothing – vest, shirt, waistcoat and, finally, a great big overcoat. When we return to higher realms we have to undress, metaphorically speaking, discarding everything which could weigh us down. Instead of working to acquire a mass of ill-assorted possessions, we must extricate ourselves from their grip and learn to do without, for an accumulation of possessions drags us downwards. Every thought, feeling or desire which is not strictly spiritual clings to us like hoar-frost on the trees of winter. We need the spring sun to shine on us, melting away the frost, exposing the true Self beneath. When we finally succeed in ridding ourselves of all our useless surplus baggage, we shall feel divine breath caressing every part of our being.

A disciple must rely on nothing, and on nobody – not even the greatest spiritual masters, nor the angels – not even the Lord Himself. The only thing we can rely on is our work, and then, because of all we have accomplished through our own efforts, we can count on the succour of the whole universe. When we plant a seed we can depend on the sun, the rain and the morning dew to make our seedlings grow. But if we have sown nothing, what can we expect? Whatever outside help we may hope for, nothing produces nothing: we would be relying on emptiness. Even God would prefer us not to lean on Him so heavily. This is why it is written: 'Strive first for the kingdom of God and his righteousness, and all these things will be given to you as well.' So it is always up to us to take the first step, to initiate the process which will give the result we desire.

You can dose a corpse with any number of medicaments, but the body will not rise up because it has lost its life. Even the most potent drugs will be of no avail if life has gone. Life is the vital component, so life must be our prime concern: we must purify and strengthen our life force so it flows freely throughout our whole being. Medicine can be a great help, as long as life flows through us. But if our body has become so sluggish that it only functions in slow motion, medicine will be of no avail: on the contrary, it will merely clog the conduits of the body. So many of us take life for granted and imagine we can live just any how. When we are sick we automatically reach into the medicine cupboard, but none of the remedies there will be really effective unless we live sensibly, nurturing the life force within.

Imagine a budding young romance: a boy and young girl begin seeing one another – they fall in love, they write to each other and exchange little gifts – a lock of hair, the tiniest flower, the petal of a rose: to them, these small offerings are talismans suffused by the ocean of their affection, bringing mutual happiness, vibrant life, and inspiration. The boy becomes a knight in shining armour, a prince, and the girl the Sleeping Beauty. They live a poetic existence, strolling arm in arm, gazing into one another's eyes, and exulting in all the beauty of the world around them. Theirs is a pure and ideal love. However, the day they feel they want to live out their love in a more physical way is the day that poetry vanishes – and is replaced by prose. You may object: 'Things aren't always ideal in this life!' but that is only your opinion. If you want to enjoy your love on a lower level you are quite free to do so, but in forsaking the realm of true poetry and true beauty, your delight will be greatly diminished. So, try to keep as much breathing space as possible in your love, for it is precisely this distance which makes the heart grow fonder: with mutual space your love will be totally fulfilling, providing a continuous source of inspiration. Thanks to this distance, your love will never die.

Even if we think we have been deprived of material advantages, we should still be able to rejoice and glorify the Lord: 'O Lord God, You are so good and so wise. You have saved me from the burden of worries and demands on my time that I would have had to endure if I had owned factories, banks or businesses. Instead, I have every opportunity to spend time thinking about You. I don't feel I am especially deserving or virtuous, because I am only satisfying my own needs, but all the same, I am so very grateful...' Just look at all those company chiefs and managing directors, forever stressed, forever rushing and agonizing over their business, teetering on the brink of nervous breakdown. Whilst you, without property, or stocks and shares, or safe-deposit in the bank, with just the bare minimum livelihood – what freedom you enjoy! For once, try to see your situation for what it really is and understand why you have been denied certain opportunities. When you resolve to examine this carefully, an inner light will shine on the situation, showing you that what you thought were hardships are actually blessings – and you will give thanks to heaven.

Clearly, our soul and spirit have nothing in common with the cosmic Soul and Spirit, but in their quintessence they are the same. This explains why our soul and our spirit must fuse with these divine entities: the eternal Masculine and the eternal Feminine. Our soul rises up to reunite with the cosmic Spirit, and our spirit is reunited with the universal Soul. In this way our two spiritual entities make exchanges with the two divine entities: the masculine part of ourselves merges with the feminine part of God, and the feminine part of ourselves merges with the masculine part of God. Not only have initiates and great mystics understood this truth, they have also devoted their entire beings to living it, and their joy knows no limit. All religions teach that we must pray to God, adore Him, and melt into Him. These prescripts are founded on the laws of our relationship with the Godhead – the relationship of our soul and spirit to the cosmic Soul and Spirit.

So many people cling on to life so desperately they even commit crimes to save their skins, because they do not know that, beyond death, a better life awaits them. So they amass huge debts which they must one day pay off. A disciple in an initiatic school sees things differently: 'Life on earth can be real drudgery. We are so limited here on earth, subject to impossible demands, ridiculed, violated and harassed. But, of course, I accept that there is always a reason for this difficulty, so I will keep working to liquidate all my debts in order to live, one day, free and unbounded in space.' Truly spiritual people know this truth, so they persist with their work here on earth, even though they know how much happier they would be in the next world. They busy themselves with paying off their debts and fulfilling the task allotted them by heaven – nothing else matters. They do not think about death, or anything else for that matter, because their work in hand is all-absorbing. And once this work has been achieved they have little inclination to stay, because they know there is not much in earthly life worth clinging on to.

When you give free rein to purely selfish, sexual desires, it is not long before you notice that certain parts of your body take on a will of their own and begin functioning independently of your own will. Then, try as you might, you are powerless to slow the pace, or stop the process: you are a mere spectator, totally lacking control. This is because you have been commandeered by other energies – entities who take over everything – and you can only watch them, powerless. Whereas, if you pursue a spiritual love, clearly it is you yourself – your soul and spirit – who are in control, and nourished. A mere glance, a presence, or a fragrance is enough to swell your hearts with happiness, because you feel your own Self – your higher Self – eating, drinking and breathing, rather than other marauding energies squatting in your body, helping themselves to all you possess.

Cutting off a part of the body to banish tormenting desire will not rid a person of that desire, because the various parts of our bodies only obey orders received from higher places. An arm, for example, can just as easily lash out at someone as give a caress: it can kill, or it can rescue. So why hold the arm responsible? The arm is not to blame, nor is it responsible for what it does: it merely carries out the orders it receives from elsewhere, both good and bad. If a man amputates his sexual organs he cannot satisfy his sexual appetite and assuage his desires, but these pangs of desire will still be there. People have been known to demonstrate their faith by mutilating themselves, to save themselves from hell – or so they thought – only to find themselves in the searing inferno of another more terrible hell. So, leave your limbs in peace and concentrate on working to purify your thoughts, your feelings, and your soul.

If we want to meditate it helps to know the nature of psychic work, and understand that we should never force the mind to concentrate too hard or too suddenly on any one idea because, if we pressurize our minds too much, we overtax our nerves and our brains seize up. So the first thing to do is relax, and stay in a passive state, like a spectator watching patiently and peacefully as our cells slowly calm down. At first this calming process may take a while, but with practice a few seconds will suffice. We must begin by working gently, peacefully, and harmoniously – this is the secret of good meditation. Then, once we feel our nervous system ready and restored – because a passive attitude allows the brain to replenish its energies – we can turn our thoughts to our chosen subject.

Work at arming yourselves with patience and love, for one day you will see your most cherished wishes come true. When will that be? It should not concern you, because it is not up to us to set a time limit to our spiritual work and exertions, and we must never do so. If you are ill, do not insist: 'I want to be cured tomorrow!' Rather say: 'Dear God, time does not matter, I accept your will, I am at your bidding. All I ask is to learn to know You and love You, and I'll wait as long as You think fit for the rest.' If we do this we shall triumph over time. But never issue orders to the Lord by setting Him a deadline for your achievement.

As soon as spring arrives we sense a stirring in everything – flowers, trees, birds. A new wave of life sweeps throughout all nature in that most extraordinary phenomenon of life: renewal. Everything renews itself, year in, year out – except for human beings, who stay exactly as they are, closed and isolated from the process of regeneration. Yet, if we want to savour the new life we must allow this life to enter and impregnate us by opening wide all the doors and windows of our being. Some say: 'But we are past all that – spring is for the young.' That sort of thinking cuts us off from the source of life. Everyone, both young and old, must flow with the tide of renewal. Here, there is no distinction between young and old. Has an old tree ever been heard to say: 'You know, we are far too old to produce flowers and green leaves, now we leave all that to the young saplings.'? People who think this way cut themselves off from the source of life. No, in spring they too cover themselves with spring foliage and blossoms. So, even old grandmothers and grandfathers must join in the dance, skipping and hopping and twirling – if only symbolically – and everything will go better.

Contrary to what many of us think, true humility is not a matter of belittling ourselves to the point of total self-effacement, continually bleating: 'I am a nobody, a good-for-nothing!' True humility is giving the Divinity pride of place in ourself, so He can manifest all His divine virtues and wealth of blessings through us. Yet who understands this? And because people have misunderstood, they reject the whole idea of humility, thinking, 'I wouldn't dream of demeaning myself!' But this attitude eventually leads them to imagine they are as important as God, and even capable of replacing Him. Little do they know this is precisely the way to degradation, to self-effacement to the point of non-existence. The greatness of each of us lies in the understanding that, despite our multitudinous grave human imperfections and shortcomings, we can achieve miracles, provided we place the Lord first in our minds and in our hearts. Without God we will not get very far – whatever we do will be prosaic and mediocre. We must understand this fact, and exert ourselves to the maximum so God can penetrate us, manifest Himself through us, and accept us into His service.

Nobody doubts that food gives energy, and everybody has heard about calories, vitamins and minerals. But has anybody taken this further, though, and wondered how food can nourish on more subtle levels? Sadly, far too few. If we were able to make ourselves truly receptive our food would tell us about the energies it contains, how these energies have travelled across the whole universe, about the beings who have encouraged its growth, and about the entities who have tended it night and day with such care and constant devotion, infusing it with the special properties for the use of God's children. Our food even bears traces of all those who worked the fields or walked nearby. Books are not the only source of learning. We can also learn from our food, and be confident that we receive living knowledge while we eat, because this food is impregnating the very substance of our whole being. Our food does not reveal its knowledge intellectually – making a poor subject for discussion – rather, we sense these revelations enhancing our whole being, enriching our entire existence.

You should not look on fasting as having to go without, or as a deprivation. On the contrary, fasting above all else serves to nourish us. Yes indeed, for when our physical bodies are deprived of food, it is our other more subtle bodies – etheric, astral and mental[1] – which begin to be nourished. We all have an instinct for self-preservation – for staying alive. If our physical bodies are not fed, an alarm goes off, and all the entities charged with watching over the survival of our organism rise to a higher region to find the missing nutriments: so our bodies begin to absorb these elements from a rarer atmosphere. Our breathing improves and, after a time, we no longer feel hungry, because we have assimilated nourishment that is not from the physical world. If we stop breathing for a few seconds, other entities from the higher astral and mental planes rush to provide all the elements necessary to keep us alive. So you see, fasting is really just another form of nutrition. Only, you must be very careful if you wish to fast, and take essential precautions: you must learn how to fast, using a great deal of wisdom – otherwise, it can prove dangerous.

---

1 See note and diagram, pages 366-367

Some people attempt to awaken kundalini by prolonged exercises of breathing and concentration, because they have read about how to become clairvoyant, or how to gain magical powers by developing their chakras. These exercises are unquestionably effective, but what is the end result? If you want to develop your chakras without any preliminary study or training, you expose yourselves to immense danger. It would be like giving a child a box of matches. What would the child do? It would start a fire. Well, you must know that kundalini, which has to be activated in order to awaken the chakras, is pure fire, and anybody who has not worked first on purity and self-mastery risks the devastating experience of witnessing the eruption of the fire of kundalini, and subsequent total inner destruction. Whereas, if you begin by working on purity and self-mastery you also work indirectly on your chakras, which will come to life and begin functioning without risk.

Life is never the same: it ebbs and flows, ever changing, moving us and everything else along in its path. Today we may feel justly proud because we have managed to solve a problem, but tomorrow another development may appear, which cannot be tackled with the same methods and approach. We constantly need to adapt our approach to each new circumstance as it arises. Know that life will always present us with different problems to resolve, and we need to find a particular, unique solution for each one. For example, yesterday a good deed or a generous gesture may have been the answer, but today another difficulty presents itself, perhaps needing the solution of reason, or action, or patience – or even by turning a deaf ear. Always, therefore, try to find the best method of dealing with every problem.

It is written in the great Book of Living Nature that our personal evolution depends crucially on the way – where, how, and for what purpose – each of us expends our energies. We have been given this energy to keep us alive, but very few amongst us take proper care of it, very few appreciate its precious value, or consider how Nature has laboured to provide it for our benefit. Many squander their energies on useless or criminal pursuits, or in sensual excesses: so these energies pour away to feed hell. Does that surprise you? Yes, human beings feed hell: through their ignorance and ill will they sustain, maintain and feed hell. That is why, if we truly wish to advance along the path of evolution, it is above all essential to watch carefully how we use our energies.

The banishing of Adam and Eve from earthly paradise is not simply the story of the misfortune of one man – Adam – and one woman – Eve, who, because they ate an apple, were guilty of disobeying God. The story of Adam and Eve tells about the mental and emotional processes at work within each individual psyche, irrespective of whether it be man or woman. When our intellect, Adam, and our heart, Eve, fail to connect with our spirit and our soul – mirror images of cosmic Spirit and universal Soul – we succumb to the lure of the lower regions. This is 'the fall'. We must therefore be on our guard not to abandon the garden of Eden – the heaven within us. To avoid falling and being engulfed by the underworld, we must hold on firmly to the world above. This may sound very complicated. On the contrary: for those who have learned to reflect and reason along the lines of the great universal symbols, it is straightforward. However, if people prefer to cling to the tale of the fellow and his wife in a garden with a snake and an apple, and if this makes sense to them and helps them evolve, then I wouldn't argue. Everybody is free to do exactly as they please.

The sun's rays can be compared to little wagonloads of victuals. They speed along to deposit their treasures with us, and then return to the sun along an invisible path. These little wagons not only carry provisions, they bring creatures who have a job to do on this earth, and then, their work done, they return sunwards to replenish themselves. The flow of the sun's rays in space is re-enacted within us. Our heart is the sun, dispatching train loads of rays throughout all the conglomerations of the physical body, distributing their load to the millions of inhabitants there. Obviously, along the way they lose some of their purity, so they cleanse themselves of all accumulated waste by following a special route back to the sun. The blood flowing through our arteries and veins replicates the radiation of sunlight throughout space: for the solar system is an organism, and the sun is its heart, and light is the blood sent out from this heart to nourish all the differing parts of the body.

During his last supper with the disciples Jesus took bread, blessed it and gave it to them, saying: ‘Take, eat, for this is my body.’ Then he took a cup of wine, blessed it, and gave it to them, saying: ‘Take this, drink it, for this is my blood. Do this in memory of me.’ The priest repeats these very same words and gestures when celebrating Communion. We cannot understand the true significance of the Mass unless we realize that the Communion is the most meaningful part of a magic ceremony, in which bread and wine represent the two eternal principles - masculine and feminine - the foundation of all creation.

Why is it that the faithful of the Catholic Church only communicate with bread - the host, Christ’s body - representing the masculine principle? Wine - the blood of Christ - representing the feminine principle, is reserved for the priests. So the faithful are nourished uniquely with the masculine principle: the feminine principle is missing. But true Communion implies the presence of the two principles, both masculine and feminine.

Christians think of the cross as a symbol reminding them of the death of Jesus: but in fact it has a far greater significance. True, it recalls the death of Jesus, but this is only one aspect. The crucifixion was a historical event, but the cross itself is hugely symbolic - a cosmic reality - and we must understand its wider importance. The widest and most profound purpose of the cross is to demonstrate the union of the two principles, masculine and feminine, and their work together throughout the universe. Another shape can be formed from this symbol: the hexagram, or Solomon's seal, made of two intertwined triangles. Here, triangles have taken the place of the straight lines of the cross, adding fresh meaning to its significance, but the idea is always the same, and the same law always applies: the work of the two principles.

The four principal feasts of Easter, Saint John, Michaelmas and Christmas take place at specific times throughout the year, and we must reflect on the universal events heralded by these feast days. Each of these celebrations corresponds to a change of season, an archangel, a planet, and a cardinal point. Easter marks the beginning of spring, under the care of the Archangel Raphael, who represents the planet Mercury, and rules over the South. The feast of Saint John marks the beginning of summer, whose fires are supervised by the Archangel Ouriel, representing Earth, ruling over the North. Michaelmas introduces autumn, under the influence of the Archangel Michael, who represents the Sun, and rules over the East. Christmas is the beginning of winter and is dedicated to the care of the Archangel Gabriel, who represents the Moon, and rules over the West. All these four major periods of the year are, therefore, the work of specific forces and beings. We, too, should at least be aware of this work, and try to participate.

Legend has it that the Grail is a cup fashioned from an emerald fallen from the forehead of Lucifer when he was thrown out into the void. This is the cup that Jesus may have used at the Last Supper, and Joseph of Arimathaea, after the crucifixion, may have gathered drops of Jesus's blood into this same cup. Joseph of Arimathaea willed it to his son. Since then, despite the vain efforts of countless people, all trace of it has vanished.

The emerald cup is the feminine principle. The colour green represents the purest aspect of Venus. It is the receptacle, the material form which collects and protects within her womb the masculine principle, the spirit, here represented by the red of blood, the colour of Mars. To initiates, the Holy Grail signifies the ideal symbol of human beings who have worked on the matter of their own bodies, purifying and rendering them incorruptible, resistant to all change, worthy of receiving that most precious quintessence of all: the Christ blood.

It is said in the Zohar: 'The Secret Book is the book of equilibrium of balance.' However, this equilibrium is not an absence of movement. When God polarized himself for the purpose of creation, the scales began to move, to sway upwards and downwards. So the act of creation implies that the two trays of the scales be in perpetual motion, and that this alternation will continue until such time as the work of creation be complete. This movement tells us that creation is continuously evolving. In fact, perfect equilibrium would block any exchange. But life is entirely dependent on reciprocal relationships. However, this movement must be measured so one side of the scales is not too high, or the other too low, otherwise that would be the end of all oscillation, and the end of all life. What we call balance is, in reality, an imbalance, an upset of equilibrium, momentarily checked, and then immediately corrected. This change in the level of the scales releases an efflux of forces, which must be rapidly balanced by a movement of contrary forces. So this fluctuation engenders life, and we can conclude that life is an imbalance continuously being rebalanced.

Whoever you are, and wherever you may be, you will encounter adversaries with whom you have to struggle. But there are two kinds of struggle: you either destroy your enemy, or you spare him. If you destroy your enemy you will no longer have to struggle, and that will prove a catastrophe as you will make no more progress. If you spare him, and have to cope with him for the rest of your life, you will become strong. Very many people try to rid themselves of their opponents, and then what happens when they succeed? They are not any happier, and because they miss the stimulus of their enemies to keep them on their toes, they feel something is lacking. So instead of destroying your foes, learn how to act to become better and stronger, and you will help your enemies at the same time. But you will succeed only if you consider them as an indispensable part of your evolution.

Many people claim to be divinely inspired. They gesticulate, rolling their eyes in all directions, holding forth incoherently, or spend hours fixed in some posture imitating a state of ecstasy. Well, these people are unbalanced and sick, and the rest of their behaviour proves it. They may talk about heaven, the holy Spirit, angels and archangels, but in fact they are really unstable. They believe they are communicating with the divine world, whereas lack of discipline and inner work has connected them with the subterranean regions of the astral[1] plane. They receive messages and commands, it is true, but they would do well to mistrust these communications. We must learn to distinguish between inspiration and various forms of mystical delirium. If we are truly in contact with heaven we receive only waves of light, harmony, and peace.

---

1 See note and diagram, pages 366-367

We owe everything to nature. She gives us all the elements that form our bodies, all the sustenance necessary to keep us alive - water, food, air to breathe, the light and heat of the sun - all the essential materials for our clothes, houses, tools, and so on. Human beings are proud of their ingenuity, but are they conscious that all the materials used to manufacture their instruments, appliances, and even works of art, are provided by nature?

Nature provides us with everything. But everything we take from nature is noted. We have incurred these debts with nature, and we must liquidate them. But how can we do so? With a payment called respect, gratitude, love, and the will to study everything written in the great book of nature. Paying means to give something in exchange, and we can do this with all that is good in our hearts, our intelligence, our souls and spirits. We are limited on the physical plane, and nature does not insist that we return all the food, water or air we have taken. But on the spiritual plane our possibilities are infinite, and it is on that level that we can repay a hundredfold all that nature has given us.

When you look after a child by caring for its soul and spirit, you attract the blessings of its guardian angel. Every small child has an angel near him, looking after him, wanting to raise his awareness, but so often this is a very difficult task because the child is subjected to such harmful, evil influences. The angel is constantly present, guarding and watching over the child, but can do very little on the physical plane, and that is why he is so very happy to see someone - a father, mother, or teacher - showing the child the way of goodness and light. The child's angel will thank such people with gifts of light and joy.

April 11

The really tragic fact about human beings is their expectation of what they will receive from others: they expect to receive what people are incapable of giving. Then, if they are given something really precious, they neglect it, because they were expecting something else. Just look around: do human beings show gratitude to their Creator? Indeed no! They even blame Him for all kinds of reasons. Are children really grateful to their parents? So often these parents are criticized and made fun of. And as for the grievances that disciples harbour towards their master, these don't bear mentioning! He may give them every conceivable method to help them work toward personal perfection, to become children of God - luminous and radiant - but it will be useless, because that is not what they expected. What they want is success, power and glory, and they blame their master most bitterly for not granting their desires. Dear Lord, what can be done with such people? It is not surprising they are forever unhappy. Let them learn to give a little in exchange for everything they have received from God, from their parents, from their master - if they have one. Let them at least find some feeling of gratitude, and they will then find peace and joy.

Human beings court misfortune because they do not see the dangers awaiting them if they make such and such a decision, or launch into such and such an enterprise. They set out so happily, blindly unforeseeing, and throw themselves head first into difficulties. If only they had known how to develop their inner vision they would have been warned, because that inner sight, known as the third eye, is like radar, sending out waves that return with warning of obstacles along the way. But most people live such disorderly lives that this radar cannot function correctly.

Sometimes it happens that this spiritual eye, however well developed it may be, does not give us due warning. The Twenty Four Elders, the Lords of our destiny, may have decreed that certain events are necessary, so these events must take place. Even though we may sense or see forthcoming trials, we cannot avoid them, and must cope with them with the light - the knowledge and methods - of initiatic science. But normally this spiritual eye is present to warn and guide us, but it can only do so if we have prepared the conditions in which it can function well.

For centuries religion has become nothing more than a series of exercises which the majority practise superficially, without any inner participation. As a result, of course, these practices have proved incapable of awakening and developing our spiritual centres: in fact, they have done the opposite, covering these centres under impenetrable layers. So now these people pray and meditate in vain, seeing and feeling nothing - neither angels, nor archangels, nor nature spirits - nothing. It never even crosses their mind that hostile entities, wanting to cause harm, may be present. Sheep feel the presence of a wolf prowling around their herd and their fear alerts the shepherds to its presence lurking nearby, so necessary precautions are taken. How can it be that sheep sense the presence of a wolf, whereas human beings have no idea that evil entities are prowling around, intent on causing harm?

Many professions are difficult, but leading human beings along the way of light and divine glory is the most difficult of all. It is a profession which demands the preparation of many incarnations - in fact it is necessary to be created specifically for such a calling. And yet, many people imagine they are capable of guiding others. They set up shop to attract disciples, to whom they deliver fine speeches. But, alas, their preparation is woefully inadequate, because it never occurs to them to begin by correcting their own many deficiencies and imperfections, and these manifest clearly in the advice, teaching and guidance they give. This is why, instead of setting their disciples on the climb up the steep tracks that lead toward sublime heights, they direct them along wandering paths scattered with treacherous pitfalls. Indeed, they themselves often fall into dire trouble.

As our physical body is constructed symmetrically on either side of a central axis - the spinal column - it has 2 sides, and can be classified as 2. We have 2 eyes and 2 ears. The brain and nose seem to be 1, but in fact are divided respectively into 2 hemispheres, and 2 nostrils. Then there are 2 lungs, 2 kidneys, and, lower down, a man has 2 testicles and a woman 2 ovaries. Finally, we have 2 arms and 2 legs.

Even though this symmetry is rarely perfect, as the left side of our bodies is never an exact replica of the right, still it remains a physical fact. But our psyche - thought and feeling - is quite different. Studies of the human brain show that the two hemispheres have different functions: the left side controls all analytical faculties - logic and reason - which can be classified as masculine qualities, and the right side is the seat of the faculties of synthesis - intuition and sensitivity - which can be considered feminine qualities. So the activities of these two hemispheres are complementary. We can therefore draw the conclusion that our physical bodies are constructed symmetrically, whereas our psyche - our thoughts and feelings - are based on the polarization of masculine and feminine - positive and negative.

To master our feelings and thoughts, we must begin by watching over our smallest everyday movements. If we do this we will, little by little, acquire the mental and emotional control that will allow us to master the most powerful of all forces. Maybe you do not see the connection - and that is exactly why you make mistakes. As long as we have not learned to master the smallest details of our daily lives we can never hope to control anger, contempt, envy, disgust, the desire for vengeance, and so on. Start by paying attention to the way you speak, and you will soon notice that you cannot even master the gestures of your hands: you wring them around, scratch yourself, fiddle with the buttons on your clothes, and so on. So, begin by learning to keep your hands still.

How can we hope to control the great forces beyond us, if we cannot yet control our tiniest instinctive movements?

Take the physical world, the spiritual world, and the divine world - or, if you like, the form, the content, and the meaning - or again, the world of action, the world of laws, and the world of principles: yes, it is always the same trinity - the body, the soul, and the spirit. The spirit is an expression of the divine world. The soul corresponds to the spiritual world. The body corresponds to the physical world. The soul, therefore, lies between matter and spirit: it is an intermediary, a vehicle that transports elements from heaven towards the earth, and from earth toward heaven. Everything that travels downwards or upwards passes through the soul. The spirit can only move downwards, and the body can only go upwards, but the soul moves up and down between the two. So, the spirit only has the power to influence matter by first passing through the soul. Observe what happens in nature: the sun cannot act directly on the earth, it needs the intermediary of air and water. In the same way, our spirit cannot influence our physical body directly, it can only act through a go-between - our soul.

Space is inhabited by billions of evil entities who have sworn to ruin humankind. Of course, there are also billions of luminous entities who work to protect and help us. Yes, but their aid will never be truly effective if we do nothing to progress along the right path. It is impossible for any master to protect us if we insist on living in an unreasonable way. A master instructs us, enlightens us, and will even try to exert an influence on us through thought and feelings. But if we destroy all his good work by opening our doors to dark entities through carelessness, stupidity, and lack of good will, what more can he do?

Many scientists believe they can justify the deadliest discoveries by the simple claim that they are working for the good of their country, and therefore fulfilling the highest moral duty. Well, in the eyes of initiatic science this claim is invalid, because this science is a universal science, which takes no account of frontiers, and is far above all forms of limitation. This science teaches the whole world the true knowledge of good and evil, morality and immorality: it states unequivocally that behaviour which is good for one country, and bad for all others, is never justifiable.

To cosmic Intelligence the essential is the goal we work towards, and how we use the talents and gifts we have been given. So, only people who make use of every one of their inner gifts in the service of the Kingdom of God are always, whatever they may do, approved, accepted and glorified on high.

Because human beings left the womb of the Eternal to undertake the long descent into matter, they need everything that matter can provide in order to stay alive. We have become so far separated from the Source, it is now impossible to return there easily and directly without making use of every available material help - machines, tools, appliances, and so on; so it is only wisdom and common sense to make full use of the many material means we have at our disposal. Only, it is important that these aids are not used to dissipate our energies and distance us even further from God. Rather, we must make use of them to return toward unity.

So what is important is our goal, our reason for using all the material advantages provided for our benefit. Whether we are eating, breathing, walking, working or loving, everything is good in so far as we mobilize everything toward our return to the divine Source.

We can never make valid judgments on good or evil, because nothing is ever either wholly good, or wholly bad. Even the best things in life bring some inconvenience. Take the arrival of spring, for example. On one hand it is marvellous - light and warmth are with us, and everything bursts into bloom. Yes, but there is another aspect: insects also flourish - wasps, flies, caterpillars, fleas and mosquitoes abound. As for technical progress, can this be classified as good or bad? Many discoveries at first bring immense improvements, but end up producing catastrophes, all because human beings have not been prudent and foresighted enough to reflect on possible future consequences. Each day produces obvious examples. So, whatever the conditions or events, precautions must be taken. The very best things may prove harmful for those who are ignorant and unprepared. On the other hand, sages know how to work, so their most difficult trials give them the means to progress.

To be simple is to know how to unify all thoughts and desires. As long as we allow free rein to all manner of thoughts and contradictory desires we will be victims of complicated and disorderly lives, and will complain: 'I don't know where I am!' This remark shows that an ill-assorted collection of desires and possessions has been accumulated, plunging us up to our necks in complications. A diamond is very valuable because it is pure carbon, without any admixture. Add another element, and it is no longer a diamond. It is the same with disciples: if they wish to taste, touch, know, and experiment with everything, they will lose their value - they will no longer be diamonds, just opaque stones. True disciples must aim for a single goal, have one ideal, one desire, and only one nourishment - symbolically speaking. If they do this, they will live in the simplicity of light.

The masculine principle is the emissive principle which projects and inseminates, providing the nucleus of life. And the role of the feminine principle is to gather up and organize the requisite materials to form something, and make it perfect. So the work of creation is spread between the two principles: we must never overestimate, or underestimate, the importance of either one. It is not appropriate to ask whether one principle is more important or necessary than the other: both are equally important, equally indispensable, but in different ways and areas. The masculine principle sends out waves, or circuits, which would be useless if the other principle were not there to respond, to receive, and to elaborate all she has received. It is these two principles that make life possible: they work together secretly and out of sight, even inside the physical body. It is only when one becomes too dominant, to the detriment of the other, that anomalies and imbalance appear. The science of the two principles is the science of cosmic balance.

Everywhere thought must come first, and must preside over everything. Everything else - feelings and desires - must take second place. Suppose you put feeling first and thought afterwards: you would be prey to instincts and inclinations, irrational and thoughtless. Yes, actions carried out in such conditions will not be much use, and may even land you in serious trouble. This does not mean that you should suppress all feeling - oh no! If you did so, you would deprive yourself of the immense wealth contained in matter, which needs to be elaborated by thought through the go-between of feeling. What is important is to put thought in first place, and then you will always find the best solutions, and the best course of action.

Do not imagine that a master, who has dedicated his life to helping human beings, does not see the bad side of their character. He sees it, and is especially skilled in detecting it, but he does not dwell on this aspect because he knows that he cannot help people by stressing only their faults and failings. In fact this attitude could even make them worse. A sage knows that men and women are all children of God, and approaches every being with this thought foremost in his mind. In this way he works as a creator, developing the divine side in everybody he meets: and he makes himself happy, also. This is the best way to deal with people: try to discover their qualities, virtues and all their inner riches, concentrate on these, and you will help them develop their gifts.

Some people consult clairvoyants to know what the future holds. Well, I should tell you that clairvoyants are not necessary, because it is all too easy to know our future. Of course, perhaps we cannot guess what our future professions, meetings, financial gains or losses, illnesses, accidents, or successes will be, but these facts are not very important. What is essential is to know whether or not we are advancing along the way of evolution, and whether we will live in freedom, light, and peace: and this is easy to discover. If you love all that is great, noble, just and beautiful, and if you work with all your heart, mind and will to realize this objective, your future is already determined: you will live, one day, in conditions which correspond to your ideal and aspirations. There! That is what you need to know about your future. Everything else is of secondary importance, because it is transient: it may be granted you, and then taken away again. When we leave the earth only the aspirations of our soul and spirit, and everything connected, truly stay with us.

The first two letters of God's name, *Iod, Heh, Vav, Heh*, יהוה represent the two great cosmic principles – masculine and feminine – which created the universe. See how expressive each of these letters is. *Heh* ה is like a receptacle or bowl, but inverted. *Yod*, י the smallest letter in the Hebrew alphabet, is hardly more than a dot or, more precisely, the germ of a seed, the primary element of a living being.

In the beginning is the *Yod*, just as in the beginning is a point. The point has no dimension and is almost impossible to define. But the movement of a point forms a line, the movement of a line produces a surface, and the movement of a surface produces volume – that is, three dimensional space. Line, surface and volume are all born of the movement of a point. Now, if you cause a line to move round the point from which it originated, you obtain a circle. The circle and its radius unite the straight line with the curved line. Thus the point is the origin of all these shapes: the point in the circle symbolizes the cosmic spirit creating life in the matter of the universe. This is the notion cabbalists express by inscribing the *Yod* within the *Heh*, thus: ה.

Get into the habit of giving the best of yourself. Obviously, this philosophy is not shared by the majority of people who have learnt only how to take: wherever they may be, this is their only thought, and their interest in others is governed by what they can get. Even in an initiatic school their motivating desire is to take: as they are totally uninterested in the truths offered them, and as there is nothing else to lay their hands on, they get bored, and leave.

From now on, this is how you must see things: imagine there is a wonderful piece of fertile ground inside you, a garden in which you cultivate all kinds of fruit and flowers, and you offer this produce as a gift for the whole world. Because you desire to do something for other people, doors open before you on to new prospects and continual new discoveries. The inner life energies spring forth only when you start giving to others, and giving of your best.

It is written in the Gospels: 'Seek and you will find. Ask and you will be given. Knock and it will be opened.' But it would be better if we could say: 'Do not seek and you will find. Do not ask and it will be given to you. Do not knock and it will be opened to you.' Does this surprise you? Of course it does, because we usually meet people who look without finding, ask without receiving, and no doors open to them when they knock. But this maxim becomes reality if we apply the Commandments and live the Christ life. Because we no longer need to ask, heaven watches over us continuously, knows what we need, and provides it spontaneously. Moreover, we do not have to continue our search because, thanks to this divine way of thinking, acting and feeling, we find truth. Finally, we do not have to continue knocking: we are living a life of perfection, so the invisible world opens every door to us, and grants us freedom.

Now that occult sciences are becoming more widespread, more and more people become interested in black magic, and as a result they begin imagining black magic all around them. When anything a little difficult or painful happens, they conclude they are being subjected to black magic. But who do they think they are? Do they imagine themselves so powerful or so dreadful that the whole world needs to join forces against them? The reality is that they are weak and ignorant. They are in the habit of frequenting the astral[1] plane and indulging sensations and emotions to such an extent that, instead of recognizing that they themselves are responsible for their sufferings, they put the blame on others. Some people have never even thought about black magic, and laugh at the idea, because they do not believe it exists. Of course, they are wrong to ignore its existence, but at least they do not blame others in the face of misfortune. These are dynamic people who, instead of trembling with fear when they are faced with difficulties, react energetically and fearlessly.

---

1 See note and diagram pages 366-367

If people took the time to reflect on the creation of the universe and all its different regions and inhabitants, they would soon realize that they are themselves an integral part of this living body of Nature.

This is why people must live in harmony with their surroundings because, if they behave like anarchists, creating upheavals everywhere, and doing nothing to make amends, Nature herself will take action because she cannot endure disharmony. It is like a tumour or a cancer and, as she knows how to defend herself, she purges herself of these excrescences. Anarchists are never tolerated for long, so if human beings do not dispatch them, Nature will.

It is, therefore, of the utmost importance that we live in harmony with this great universe upon which we depend for food and shelter.

Everybody is a living being, of course, but most live vegetative, animal, emotional, or even intellectual existences. On the higher spiritual plane many are already dead, and when one is dead spiritually it is only a short time before one dies on a lower level. They say that a fish starts to rot in its head. This happens to people who allow their heads to decay – meaning to abandon the spirit: the decay ends up by spreading to every cell in the body. Once people die spiritually, they die in other regions[1], one after the other: on the mental plane they lose their light, on the astral plane their warmth, and on the etheric plane their vital energies. Then, no longer supplied by these energies, the physical body dies. When an initiate talks about life he always means spiritual life, because this is what supports the whole human edifice.

1 See note and diagram pages 366-367

There are events which people cannot avoid because everything written in their destiny must take place, so in this sense they are not free. If we live reasonably we are granted only one freedom: we are permitted to pay our karmic debts in some way other than previously decreed. For example, suppose we are to be gravely ill and laid low for some time: this illness is a debt that has to be paid for some past transgression. But the debt can be paid in a different way by undertaking some serious spiritual work of prayer and meditation. Therefore, when our illness comes it will be less serious, since part of our debt has already been paid with our work of light and love, and we shall be out of action for only a few days. Our spiritual efforts have strengthened our organism. The same principle applies to all trials of life. The moment we encounter a difficulty caused by some planetary aspect, or the transit of some planet through our astrological chart, if we have already done serious spiritual work, accumulating 'money' – forces and energies – towards the settlement of our debts, we can confront our trials in the best possible conditions.

The Creator has placed within us a great variety of seeds – qualities, faculties and gifts – and if these have not yet sprouted, it is because they have not yet been watered, or received the light and warmth of the sun. To all those who question whether these seeds are real, I say: 'Go to the Sun, and he will shine his light on them and make them grow and blossom. Then you will doubt no longer.' But when I talk about the Sun, about how he develops our inner seeds, understand that I am referring to the spiritual Sun. The physical sun is no more than an image to help us understand how these phenomena occur on the spiritual plane.

Each of the seven colours of the prism corresponds to a virtue: violet to sacrifice, indigo to strength, blue to truth, green to hope, yellow to wisdom, orange to holiness, and red to love. But it is almost useless to work to obtain spiritual powers with light and colours, unless we also work on the corresponding inner virtues. Similarly, all those who imagine that they are going to become great sages merely by performing rituals or evoking spirits, without improving their inner life in any way, are greatly mistaken. Higher beings are not deluded by such attempts. These people have merely succeeded in summoning lower beings – elementals and monsters – from the depths. If you want to attract angels and archangels, you can do so only by acquiring virtues, because the highest entities only frequent those who manifest true light: the light of purity, love, wisdom and truth.

People come to see me and ask: ‘Master, I would like you to tell me about my weaknesses and the faults I have to correct?’

– ‘Are you sure you're not going to be upset?’

– ‘Oh no! I will take your advice.’

Hardly have I started to speak when, sure enough, the tears pour down. As a result I have to stop, because if they are so overcome by emotion and distress they are incapable of even listening, let alone understanding. To understand, we must silence our emotions. If we are in a state of distress and vexation, how can we understand? So many people, face to face with someone capable of enlightening them, over-react, offended and hurt. This is not intelligent. At least once in a lifetime we must make up our minds to accept certain truths, even if they are unpalatable, because it is precisely these truths which help us solve our problems.

If we do not possess the qualities we wish to awaken in others, however hard we try, all our efforts will be doomed to failure. Nothing external can change human beings. I repeat, you must understand that there are no available external means with which to transform people. Some special element must be emanated from your heart, soul and spirit which vibrates, and has the power to influence other people to imitate you: without any special effort on your part, people will want to be like you. Perhaps this may not happen all at once because they cannot, overnight, get rid of all their inferior instincts and desires, but they will realize that you do have some luminous, warm and vibrant quality, and it is this light, warmth and vitality they find compelling.

Every night, before you go to bed, gather your thoughts briefly, and leave aside everything that preoccupied or troubled you during the day. Then think of any possible mistakes, and ask the luminous spirits to show you the best way to redress these during your sleep. Finally, just as you are about to sleep, place yourself under the protection of the Angel of Death. The Angel of Death is the name given by the Cabbala to the Angel of Sleep, because every night we die and every morning we come to life again. Sleeping, which is merely leaving our physical body, is a practice for when we finally leave for the other world. The person who does not know about the process of sleep will not know how to cope with dying. There is no difference between sleep and death, except that when we die we leave the house in which we used to live. This is why we must prepare for sleep every night as if for a sacred journey, so we are ready for the day when we will set out on that other, much more conclusive journey: death.

In the everyday world a boss can often be hard, overbearing or unjust: he takes decisions, makes demands, criticizes and orders people about. He is never satisfied. He has only developed one side of his nature: the demanding and authoritative. He sees only his personal interests and does not want to be bothered with the plight of his subordinates.

On the other hand, a master in an initiatic school, a true master, is a servant of God. He has trodden the path of service and he continues to serve. He has learnt how to obey and how to master himself. He can empathize with his disciples because, in times past, he has already been through, and achieved, all that he now expects of them. He is fully aware of all he is doing, as he well knows the difficulty, and value, of everything he expects from his disciples.

It is astonishing how many people believe they have been entrusted with some special mission. God has chosen them, it seems, to save their country, to fight dissidents and heretics, to purify the earth, and so on. Yes, there are, unfortunately, a great many people ready for such false missions, but candidates for life's true mission are few and far between.

– 'What is this true mission?' you ask.

– 'Be ye perfect even as your heavenly Father is perfect.' is the goal Jesus urges each and every human being to work towards.

True disciples of the Universal White Brotherhood undertake first and foremost to fulfil this mission: we must work on ourselves until we achieve perfection. But since we cannot do this in such a short lifetime, we shall return and reincarnate to continue this great work. It is only by patient, sustained work on ourselves that the Kingdom of God will come on earth: certainly not by the intervention of the handful who imagine they have been entrusted with some special heavenly mission.

Whatever work you have to do you must always use the requisite tools and techniques. This seems obvious, yet some spiritualists, instead of simply putting the food they want to eat on the table, may go into a state of intense concentration to 'spirit' the food out of the cupboards. Instead of exerting themselves by putting their arms and legs, eyes, ears and mouth to use to obtain all their material needs, they prefer to bother heaven with their petty requirements. This behaviour does not please heaven. These people have been given every material advantage but, despite this, they demonstrate only ignorance and indolence.

The quest for light, wisdom, peace or love demands the use of our mental faculties – meditation, prayer and contemplation: but to obtain our material requirements we have to roll up our sleeves and get to work.

When teachers complain, as they often do, of being tired and worn out, it is not because looking after children is in itself tiring. It is because they tend to have a mercenary attitude, looking on their career first and foremost as a means of earning money: this is their main preoccupation, not the children, so they hurry to finish their work and be free. Of course, children are often a handful: but if you decide on the teaching profession, the children's future must be your prime concern, and you must cherish them with loving care. As children are sensitive to love and tenderness, after a time they will become quite transformed.

This holds true for teachers, and parents also. Whether teacher or parent, it is essential to have the right attitude towards children. However, to achieve this, it may be better to stop concentrating solely on the children, and try instead to concentrate on yourself and the qualities you need to cope with your role: instead of being continually exasperated, with nerves stretched to the limit and on the floor with exhaustion, try to be calmer, more attentive, patient and loving, and you will find you have far more energy.

Wisdom is gold – gold from the sun. Yes, wisdom, spiritual gold, comes from the sun. With this gold you can buy anything in the world of the soul and spirit, in exactly the same way as physical gold can buy you anything you want on earth. When you enter a boutique in heaven, if you can show you have spiritual gold in your bank, you will be showered with generous supplies of all you need, and will leave with laden shopping bags.

At sunrise we collect gold, little glittering flakes of gold, thanks to which we can buy anything in heaven – love, joy, expansion, and abundance. Sometimes people who are ignorant of the supreme importance of earning spiritual gold, and have no idea of the value of watching the sun rise every morning, poke fun at us, calling us ‘sun worshipers’. Well, perhaps they have plenty of money in their banks at the moment, but sooner or later they will go bankrupt, in spite of all their millions, because they are unaware of the value of spiritual gold.

May 19

Sometimes I am asked to explain to people why, during meditation, they experience the disturbing feeling of being uncontrollably swept face to face with something terrifying. As they obviously do not understand this phenomenon, I explain: having left their physical body, they drifted into the obscurity of the lower astral regions[1], where they experienced this frightening sensation of being pursued and threatened. Encounters in the astral plane are not always reassuring. If you have a similar experience during your meditation, react quickly and return at once into the shelter of your physical body. Prolonging this experience could be fatal, so do not let curiosity tempt you to explore this new and unknown realm. Make every effort to return into your body as quickly as possible, because you are not yet strong enough to confront the entities of the astral plane.

---

1 See note and diagram, pages 366-367

Once upon a time there was a kingdom where disasters continuously swept the land – famine, riots and epidemics. The king, at his wits' end, sent for a sage who told him: 'Majesty, you are the cause of all these misfortunes: you live a life of debauchery, and you are cruel and unjust. That is why your people continuously suffer from all these catastrophes.' The sage then addressed the people: 'If you are suffering, this is because you have deserved it: you live in a senseless way, so you have attracted a monarch who is responsible for all your troubles.' This is how sages explain such things. When a whole nation decides it wants to live in the light, heaven will send noble and honest leaders who will bring nothing but blessings. But if a people is governed by rulers incapable of deciding what is best for their prosperity and well being, the people must accept that it is mainly on their own shoulders that the responsibility for their plight rests.

Whenever you have to deal with an important problem, find a quiet spot where you can be alone and, in the silence, concentrate your thoughts. Use your thoughts to rise very high, to that point where you sense your question will be heard, ask your question, and then wait peacefully. A reply will always come. However, the clarity of this answer depends on your degree of spiritual evolution: maybe it is just a vague sensation, difficult to interpret, but at least it is an indication. So, don't give up: link up again with the world of light, pose your question once more, and soon afterwards a sensation of clarity and certainty will permeate you. Doubt and uncertainty are dispelled. You know exactly what to do. The more we are developed spiritually, the clearer and more precise our answers will be.

Every night we undress before going to bed. We take off our clothes one after the other – pullover, shirt, vest, and so on. Well, this undressing symbolizes death; the clothes taken off represent the different bodies from which we have to free ourselves, one after the other. Conversely, when we wake up in the morning we put our clothes on again – vest, shirt, and so on – symbolizing the involution of the spirit. When the spirit descends into matter it begins by clothing itself with its more subtle bodies – atmic, buddic and causal – then with the increasing density of the mental, astral and etheric bodies, and finally with the physical body. Every night we get undressed, and every morning we get dressed again. You have probably been doing this for years without a thought for the significance of this habitual action. From now on, be very conscious of the implication of these mundane gestures, and be aware that they reflect the whole process of incarnation and disincarnation.

The descent of the holy Spirit into humankind is a symbolic event which all religions recognize, and very few of us understand, because of our tendency to consider the holy Spirit as an entity separate from us. This is not so: the holy Spirit is not an external and alien entity. When we receive the holy Spirit it is our own spirit, or higher Self, that takes possession of us.

The higher Self is always ready and waiting to enter and take possession of us, but our impurities block the way. If we can work on purifying ourselves thoroughly, one day we will achieve a true state of holiness, and the holy Spirit will descend and enter us. The holy Spirit is our higher Self – powerful, luminous, radiant, and capable of accomplishing wonders.

For optimum health, people need to live in conditions which help reinforce their defence systems: in other words, in a place where they can increase their life energies. This is the best medicine. Yes, only the life-force is all-powerful – see how life heals wounds, cleans abscesses, and prompts nails, hair and new skin to grow. And yet this life, which is so precious, is the thing we neglect most. People lead such chaotic and disordered existences that they ruin themselves, draining their energies to such a pitiful degree they are unable to cope with even the smallest upset. They resort to pills and tablets, but these dead substances can do nothing to make them feel better. You can warn them, 'Take care because you are ruining your life!' but this warning will fall on deaf ears. 'What do you mean? Life is for living!' Agreed – providing life's energy is used reasonably, and not squandered.

The traumas of life – such as disease, suffering, and other trials – force people to make progress. What is war, for instance? It is an imbalance which the good use to become even better, and the bad to become worse. Life creates these disturbances, this disequilibrium, forcing us to evolve and transform ourselves, or, at the least, to reveal our true selves. Without trials or dangers, many of us would never have the chance to learn our true potential. This explains the behaviour of those who, apparently honest, capable and intelligent, are immediately transformed into terrible cowards or criminals under the pressure of trials and danger. On the other hand, in the same difficult conditions, apparently insignificant people can conduct themselves like heroes or saints.

Anyone wishing to advance along the path of evolution must start by developing an awareness of the invisible world. But this is only a preliminary. We may accept that entities exist in space, and inside us, and that energies circulate around and within us, but that is not enough: we must make an effort to collaborate with these entities and energies in order to work constructively together. Our homes, offices, and personal appearance – everything in the physical world – may be in immaculate order, and that is excellent. But inside, our thoughts and feelings may be in total disarray, because it has not occurred to us that these thoughts and feelings exist in a world that is a reality, and it is important to work in this world to create order, harmony and beauty. From now on, change your attitude: recognize the reality of the invisible world – a reality far more important than the visible world – and concentrate on looking after it, above all else.

Whenever we meet acquaintances, or strangers, we make contact with our hands – by waving or shaking hands. But hands not only relate us to other people, they can also provide a link with Nature. When you open your window or front door in the morning, get into the habit of greeting the whole of nature, trees, sky and sun and say 'Good morning' to the whole of creation. 'What is the use of that? Is it helpful?' you may ask. Yes, it is: our whole day depends on this first essential gesture, which links us to the source of all life. The whole natural world will open itself to you in response to your greeting, and send you supplies of energy the whole day through.

Initiates place the masculine principle before the feminine principle, not because they consider it more important, but because they respect cosmic hierarchy. Symbolically, the masculine principle represents the spirit – the first quintessence of all creation, which works on matter – represented by the feminine principle. Each needs the other: the spirit needs to incarnate in matter, and matter needs to be given life by the spirit. Creation is none other than the result of this union of spirit with matter. In family life a father's role and responsibility is no more, or less valuable, than the mother's. They both are equally valuable and important, because both are necessary for the creation of a child.

What science calls 'the evolution of the species' was necessarily preceded by a movement of involution, for there can be no upward movement unless something has already descended. For the spirit to rise toward heaven, it must first have descended from heaven, the source and origin of all being. This is true of physical matter. It is also true of all that exists, including human beings. The theory of evolution advanced by Lamarck and Darwin accounts for only fifty per cent of reality. Before there can be evolution of matter there is involution of the spirit. Evolutionists see things only from the outside, from the point of view of the organization of matter, and fail to take into account the invisible forces that fashioned matter in the first place. Evolution is only one half of the process of manifestation. When one studies this half in isolation one cuts it off from the truth of life and removes it from its rightful place in nature. It can never be proved that a process of evolution is possible, unless it is set in motion and sustained by an initial impulse. Of course, this impulse comes from above. The initial movement is that of the spirit which descends, and if we see that matter evolves it is because it is being carried upward, back to its source, by the ascending movement of the spirit.

A magus is a medium who provides the raw material the entities of the invisible world need to make contact with the physical plane, and act on it. These invisible entities are attracted by the fluidic emanations released by his concentration and activities, because they need them to adopt physical shape, and be active in the material world. But the mere presence of a criminally motivated being releases putrid fumes, attracting swarms of dark spirits who hurl themselves on these stinking emanations, so necessary for their evil purpose. It is not the person himself who acts harmfully, he merely furnishes other entities with the means and materials for their evil work. Conversely, the presence of a white magus provides luminous spirits with everything necessary to proliferate blessings far and wide. Do you wish to work for the light, and do good? Then, already, you are releasing a substance of great purity, and heavenly entities are gathering it up exactly like bees gathering nectar from flowers to make honey.

It is written in the Gospel: 'Walk while you have the light, so that darkness may not overtake you. If you walk in the darkness, you do not know where you are going.' Light allows us to get our bearings and to find what we are looking for. Many people seek God sincerely, that is true, but they do it in the night: they want to see the sun, symbolically speaking, but after it has set, so they have no hope of finding what they seek. Having looked around for a while they come to the conclusion that there is no sun. They claim this is corroborated by the evidence of forty or fifty years painstaking observation, and as death approaches they say: 'The sun does not exist. I never found it.' People nowadays are all busy looking in the dark, and this fact seems to be the hallmark of contemporary culture. People do not find the sun, the meaning of life in other words, because they lead a nocturnal life and they go to bed when the sun rises… to avoid seeing it at all.

Outwardly, most of us are perfectly decent people. We have never broken society's laws for fear of being caught and convicted: yet we have no qualms at all about disobeying divine laws, although these laws are in fact far more ruthless. If we are intelligent, or perhaps just lucky, we can always evade human laws. As for divine laws, no one has as yet been able to evade those, however intelligent or clever he or she may be. Over and above us and our minor intelligence there exists a far greater intelligence which watches and records everything, and that is why those who do wrong are always found out and punished. Unwittingly, they always leave traces behind somewhere. Even a thought or a feeling leaves traces. We go out somewhere, and would seem to be behaving impeccably, and outwardly this may be so, but if inside we have criminal thoughts, these thoughts will be recorded in the subtle world. That is why divine law will pursue us, and some time later those delinquent thoughts will in one way or another return, with dire consequences.

People must become more and more aware that they have at their disposal faculties which are far superior to their intellect. Our intellect is a tool which serves us well for studying or exploring matter, but otherwise it is not a very good guide, even in our everyday lives. For not only does the intellect only give a partial perception of reality, it also, in all that it undertakes – and this is even more important – has a hidden motive, and makes self-centered calculations which will always create trouble. If we are ruled by our intellect, whenever we make a sacrifice or a generous gesture, we immediately wonder whether we have acted correctly, thinking how foolish we have been to listen to our heart and soul.

Moreover, the intellect is not capable of conceiving the idea of brotherhood amongst all peoples, of everybody on earth forming one family, of the whole world living together in peace and harmony. It cannot elevate itself high enough to discover true remedies, and true solutions. Partial and selfish, the intellect's vision and counsel are invariably wanting in some way, and can only cause misunderstanding.

Do not imagine that, simply by following a spiritual teaching, all your problems will be solved. No! Far from it. In order to sort out our problems, we must set out a precise inner goal, and draw up a programme of work to achieve this goal. Once we have defined our targets, regardless of whether we have achieved them or not, at least these defined aims will have made an impression somewhere within us, and our subconscious forces are then obliged to circulate through the conduits formed by these intentions. If nothing is prepared beforehand in this way, the whole of our life passes by without achievements of any kind whatsoever. When rain falls, water is channelled along the gullies we have dug. We must therefore prepare the ground, digging out watercourses so that new life may circulate within us.

Your children are dreams, thoughts and feelings that you have had in the past, and which you have now clothed in physical form. You do not know who you were in the past? Well, look at your children and they will tell you: 'Watch us, we are here to show you what you were really like.' If you want to know the truth about people all you have to do is look at their children. You will tell me you are not married and you have no children – but, there again, you are mistaken. Your children can also be your actions, and that is how, each and every day, you bring children into the world. Jesus said that you can tell a tree by its fruit. If your fruit is tart, bitter and acidic, it proves that within you, the mother – the heart, and the father – the intellect, are defective. Action is a child, and this child can only be divine if this inner father and mother have conceived it divinely.

It is customary in every country to bring gifts to those we visit. It is a very old tradition based on the law of never going to visit anyone empty-handed. You should always go to meet someone wishing to bring them something. It is also important not to greet someone with an empty vessel or container because, if you do, you bring that person emptiness for the rest of the day. When you go to meet friends never hold an empty basket, bucket or bottle. If you really must hold a container (basket, bag, bucket, and so on) then put something in it before you set out – this need not be anything precious, perhaps just water, which is the most precious substance in the eyes of the Creator: then you can go to meet your friends knowing that you are bringing them health, joy, fulfilment, and an abundance of every blessing.

Thanks to our subtle bodies[1] we human beings are in touch with the entire cosmos, living and vibrating as one with the universal Soul, and with each generation, reaching back to the furthest distant past. We are in contact with the world of ideas, archetypes, laws, forces, and truths, and this world can manifest itself in us in the form of images and symbols. If we meditate on the very high truths of the causal plane, there is a movement in the depths of our subconscience, and instantly a shape appears: either in the form of a being, an object, or a geometric figure. This is the explanation of premonitory dreams and prophetic visions. Left to yourselves you would never find a precise explanation: you would never manage to find the exact corresponding sign, because thousands of symbolic forms exist. Nature alone holds the key to the affinities between all things; so she presents an image before our inner spiritual eye which matches perfectly the object of our concentration.

---

1 See note and diagram pages 366-367

A man lies stretched out on the floor: you can see him, you can even touch him, but he is obviously dead. He is there, but lacking something invisible: that something which enabled him to walk, talk, love and think, has gone. You can offer him all the food or treasure in the world, putting it beside him, coaxing him: 'Have a good time with all this, my friend!' but it won't do any good, because nothing can persuade him to budge. How, then, can people question the existence of an invisible world? The body before us – the visible world – is nothing if it is not animated and sustained by the invisible world. We must always seek the invisible beyond the visible. If the world exists for us, if we can see the sky and sun, it is only because of this invisible principle within which allows us to discover all we see by means of these visible instruments – our eyes. Were it not for the existence of that invisible principle, our physical eyes would be useless, and we would see nothing. The visible world is only the outer covering of the invisible world, and without this invisible element we would know nothing of all that exists around and about us.

The skin, the ears, the eyes and the nose are all organs that allow us to come into contact with the physical world; if one of these is impaired, we are not able to do our work properly. And what is true for the physical plane is also true on the spiritual plane. If we have not managed to develop the organs we need to make contact with the spiritual world, we have no means of getting to know it. And this is the case for most human beings; they have not yet developed those necessary organs and that is why they are content to say: 'If I don't feel it, it doesn't exist.' This, despite the fact that regular scientific devices have made clear for a long time that there are innumerable sound and light vibrations both within, and beyond, our capacity to perceive them. People's perceptions are therefore limited, but their reasoning is even more limited. The time has come, therefore, for them at least to recognize their limitations: because to deny the existence of what cannot be heard with their physical ears, or seen with their eyes, can only retard their evolution.

Instead of spending all your time reading, and running hither and thither always chasing some new thing to learn, get into the habit of setting aside a few moments every day to connect with the divine world. What you will gain from this practice you will be able to take with you wherever you go, even into the other world: nothing will be able to take it away. Everything you find in books, all the knowledge that you are able to acquire, you will never truly possess: when you leave this earth you will have to abandon it all, and when you come back you will have to start learning all over again. When you come into this world you bring with you only what you, yourself, truly acquired: you are stripped of all the rest because you took it from others, so it did not belong to you. All you have borrowed will of course bring you earthly benefits for the brief period you spend on this earth – you will be complimented, lauded and applauded by people who are not very enlightened. But when you depart this world you will be naked and destitute. And when you return to earth you will find yourselves in the same state of nakedness and poverty.

The truth is, the spirits of human beings are not yet truly established in their bodies. The spirit is dragged along, buried, crushed, sometimes even suffocated, but never established in the body. The spirit can only establish itself in a home that is worthy of him. In the meantime the spirit, or rather what is thought of as the spirit, ambles along with the body, zigzagging unsteadily like some fellow arm in arm with his girl. What a sight! That, however, is exactly the situation of human beings who have not yet understood that they have to work on themselves. And what is that work? It is to free the divine principle within, so that he may rise as high as possible, and then, descending from the heights, he returns to purify and illuminate his own dwelling. This dwelling is our physical body, but also our astral and mental[1] bodies, through which our spirit must be able to manifest one day.

---

1 See note and diagram pages 366-367

Many philosophers, poets and mystics have said that life is a dream. It is not because life is a dream, however, that we should allow ourselves to indulge in daydreaming, as so many do. They want this, they wish for that, but these rambling incoherent dreams, with neither head nor tail, inspired only by sensuality, whims or laziness, are not to be recommended. One can dream, of course, one *should* even dream, but only if the dreams are conscious, divine, and always directed toward the good and the light: in other words, toward the Kingdom of God on earth, where all beings are living in love and peace, free at last. If more men and women often dreamed like this, they would quickly make their dreams come true. It is up to each one of us to create the sublime images that will bring about the transformation of the human race.

How free you are depends on which rung you have reached on the ladder of evolution. If you are at the bottom of the ladder you have no freedom. Are animals free? Or plants? Or stones? Even among human beings, many are not free: they are pressured and influenced by other people, or by entities from the invisible world. Their decisions are not their own. In order to be free you must rise up to the Lord. It is at the top that you are free, and nowhere else. Only the Lord is free. All other creatures are not free: not even the archangels, as they are immersed in the soul of the Lord, and receive His influence. They are free through the freedom of the Lord, but they are not free in relation to the Lord. Only the Lord is free, and all creatures are free through His freedom only to the extent that they draw close to the Lord: but not in any other way.

You make plans for a trip, a joint venture or moving house. Even if you consider these plans to be eminently sensible in reality there is something that will always escape your notice: that 'something' is the long-term consequences of your undertaking.

You may wish to discredit someone you consider a competitor, a rival, or an opponent, and you may succeed: but in fact you cannot know if you have caused any real harm. Despite having been the target of hurtful intentions, many have ended up, through a whole chain of circumstances, being successful and happy.

Good and evil ... we have to wait before we can evaluate this question correctly because only time can tell what is good and what is bad. There is only one way to reach an understanding of this: it is to examine the events of our own lives, and throughout the history of the human race.

Jesus said: 'This is eternal life: that they may know you, the only true God, and Jesus Christ whom you have sent.' In order to know the Lord you must unite with Him. Fusion, however, is not possible between objects made of different materials or densities. For instance, if you scatter a few droplets of mercury and then push them back together, they re-form into one drop. No doubt you have all tried that experiment. Supposing, however, you scattered dust on these droplets: try as you might, they will stay separate. And that is what happens with us. The Lord is of such splendour, such purity, such immensity, how could we fuse with Him if we remain impure, depraved and malicious? That is why we must always try to purify ourselves, to eliminate all the layers of dirt that prevent fusion. And self-purification means making sacrifices and renouncements, learning self-discipline and self-mastery. Then we can communicate with divine vibrations and, thanks to our pure, intense life, we can secure these vibrations within us.

People tend to concentrate solely on the gain of external acquisitions, in any and every sphere. They do not see the futility of wanting to own objects which are outside of them, which can never really belong to them. As long as people have money, machines, weapons and so on, they feel strong, and confident that everything is going well. The day they are deprived of all these, however, they feel completely lost.

A disciple of initiatic science has come to understand this very well, so he works on his inner strengths and wealth: and in this way his weapons, his wealth and his blessings belong to him throughout eternity.

Initiates are not against new technological discovery. Indeed, they also use these discoveries, and are very pleased to have them: however, they know how to avoid the trap. They work in a different sphere which belongs to them, and they can resort to it at any time. That is true independence.

People tend to let themselves go when external conditions are comfortable. They need to have problems and misfortune to oblige them to get a grip on themselves, to make efforts to put right the situation. And when they have succeeded in doing so, they give up trying, and slump back into laziness. Well – this is not the right attitude. Whatever the external situation may be, we must always continue to work, knowing that work must always take first place. Good material conditions must not be an excuse for letting ourselves go. It is the exact opposite. We must learn to use these good conditions by setting aside more time for working with thought, to the construction of our inner being.

Of course, every person is an individual, independent and autonomous. But every person is also part of the human collectivity and, still further beyond, of all the realms of nature, of the cosmic collectivity. We therefore live two lives simultaneously: both a personal life and a collective life. Most people are not really aware of all this, but they would do well to make it a conscious fact. If you seek to immerse yourself in collective, universal life, you must not lose sight of your own personal existence because, if you do, you would be thinking and acting irresponsibly. Equally, if you feel you are an individual totally separated from everybody else, it is important to realize, whilst retaining the feeling of unique individuality, that you belong to a whole, that you are a cell in a social organism, and beyond that, a cell in the cosmic organism.

It is said that God humbles the proud and elevates those who are humble. All those who rely only on themselves under the pretext that they have some intellectual powers are, in reality, arrogant: they rely too much on their limited brains, so the Lord cuts them down in size by taking away some of their capabilities. Whereas those who do not have this absolute confidence in themselves and say to the Lord: 'You alone have light and knowledge. Enter inside me, Lord, inspire me!' – it is they who are truly humble. This humility makes them more clear-headed and more intelligent, and the mysteries of the universe begin to be revealed to them.

Pride is a fault of the intellect. Those who rely too much on their way of seeing and understanding are arrogant. They never consider the possibility of another point of view, or think they could be mistaken. Oh no! They are perfect. Well, that attitude is extremely detrimental, because over the years it diminishes their mental capacity and ossifies their thinking.

People detest each other, and speak ill of each other: of course, they know full well that such conduct is not consistent with the teaching of the Gospels, but they don't seem to care. What they do not realize, however, is that a law exists according to which those who incessantly speak ill of others are, in doing so, actually handing over their own strength, and giving appropriate weapons for retaliation: they themselves are actually empowering their enemies. Do you want to disarm your enemy? If so, say good things about him, find at least one good quality and tell others about it. Then the spirits will go to him and ask how much credit he has in his bank. 'Very well,' they will say, 'You owe some to that person, over there, because he has said good things about you.' Speak ill of him, however, and the spirits will come and force you to settle the score by paying out your own energies; so it is you yourself who give strength to your enemy.

Sometimes a particle of dust, a hair, a thread or a blade of grass gets into a piece of equipment, or machine, and stops it working. Yes, the machine itself is intact, with all its working parts, but the smallest thing is enough to put it out of order. As for you, there you are with your head, your arms, your legs and your organs, all present and correct – nothing is missing: but perhaps your neighbour did not say hello in passing, or you did not get the reply you expected, or a friend said something hurtful, or the dentist or the hairdresser kept you waiting longer than expected – the list of all these minor everyday hiccups is endless – and there you are, in a bad mood for the rest of the day. These are tiny specks of dust but they are enough to make everything in your mental, emotional and spiritual world grind to a halt. So think: is it really worth ruining an entire day for something so trivial? Learn to blow away the dust and you will feel so much more light-hearted, so much more at peace.

Magic is nothing more than the the laws of physics applied to the spiritual world. One of these laws reveals the power of the rays of the sun when concentrated on a single point: they produce fire. In the same way, spiritual physics teaches us that people, also, can use their thoughts to produce the same effect as sunbeams. If you learn to concentrate your mind on a precise point you can generate much good for the world. There may not be much to see on the physical plane, but on the etheric, astral, and mental[1] planes, your concentration of thought will have burnt away many impurities.

---

1 See note and diagram pages 366-367

We have a tendency to think of ourselves as the centre of the universe. So a master – whose only concern is for our future and our evolution, spending his whole life, and all his time and energy to be of service to us – is obliged to remind us of our rightful place. However, instead of understanding that he is doing so for our own good, we are offended, hurt, or even outraged. This is not the right attitude to adopt. If you are always listening to your lower nature, which wishes the whole world to revolve around it, you should realize it can only give you the wrong advice. So why persist with this attitude? When your master tries to quell your baser instincts, give him a hand instead of howling in protest. By protecting your lower nature you destroy the work of your master who only wants to help you. Work with him. If he knocks your personality about a little, commend him. When your lower nature sees that no-one is on its side, it will finally admit defeat.

The masculine principle is defined as active, and the feminine principle as passive, but passivity plays just as important a role as activity. Whereas the masculine principle provides the content, the feminine principle provides the container, or form. This form is endowed with a tremendous power of attraction. We define the feminine principle as passive in order to distinguish from the active masculine principle. In reality the feminine principle is not inactive: she exerts an action and this action, which takes on the appearance of passivity, is extremely effective. Instead of projecting herself forward, like the masculine principle, the feminine principle attracts towards herself. That is what she does, and he who is not truly able to resist her is absorbed. Masculine activity is more visible, but it is not more powerful. In a sense, being active is to move from the centre towards the periphery, whereas being passive is to attract elements from the periphery toward the centre. And even if this attraction is not very apparent, it is real and powerfully active.

To describe someone as 'well-balanced' is to acknowledge that they have one of the most precious qualities, and one of the most difficult to acquire, because it is the result of two contradictory movements. Some people seem to feel good and find life so effortless, judging by the way they occupy themselves with talking, walking, and going about their daily lives. We could say these people are well-balanced, but in fact they are not: they are stagnating. Day after day they are always the same, as if an inner spring had lost its tension. They always wear the same impassive expression, go through the same stereotyped motions, and they repeat the same phrases, day after day. They cannot evolve in this way.

We need a certain amount of imbalance to progress, but only provided we keep a close watch on ourselves and know how to correct the scales when they become too lopsided. Knowing how to keep different forces in balance gives us a magical power over ourselves and over nature, but we must watch carefully to maintain a certain amount of movement to and fro. If ever the scales stop in perfect balance, all movement stops and death sets in. Indeed, death is perfect balance.

Therefore, we must always be making adjustments. The true quality of 'good balance' is the most difficult state of all to attain.

When we pray, when we meditate, our soul is drawn toward the universal Spirit and our spirit is attracted by the universal Soul, and when they meet we experience an overwhelming sense of fulfilment. This meeting is what makes our prayers and meditation so meaningful. Why pray, otherwise?

Prayer is different from sending the Lord a list of requirements such as, 'I need this. I want that.' Prayer enables us to find the true dimensions of our being. That meeting between something within us and something of the same nature in the universe is what gives meaning to our prayer and all our spiritual exercises. There is an encounter, a meeting of two polarized entities. This encounter is religion's greatest secret: the human soul in search of the divine Spirit, and the human spirit in search of the universal Soul. Our soul is fertilized by the cosmic Spirit, and our spirit fertilizes the universal Soul. This is the way we become true creators.

Everything in existence attracts a little dust or grime in the course of time. A house, however special and beautiful it may be, always ends up being invaded by dust and cobwebs if it is not cleaned regularly. The same applies to our body, which must be cleaned and purified in order to ensure that no dust or cobwebs of any kind oppose the work of the higher entities, who bring the life of the divine world to us. That is why we must regularly, every day even, think not only of clearing our stomachs, our lungs and our brains, but also our heart, our will and our intellect, of all the elements that cause decay and prevent us from vibrating in harmony with celestial realms.

The lower nature and higher nature are so inextricably linked in human beings that it is impossible to say where one ends and the other begins. Divinity lives in all human beings, even the least evolved: the difference lies in the level of consciousness. God lives in the most ordinary person in the same way and with the same degree of completeness as He does in a spiritual master, but the ordinary person stops the Divinity from manifesting because he does not realize that God is already within him. There are people in whom the divine Presence does not manifest, because they refuse to accept It, so they cannot receive It. God lives within us, and He wants to manifest Himself in all His beauty, His power, His light and His love. It is therefore up to us to become conscious of this Presence and to work at making It live within us in all Its splendour.

People are so appreciative of gold and so eagerly search for it because, subconsciously, they know a secret. This secret is that gold is a condensation, a materialization of the light given out by the sun, and this light contains life, strength – everything. Before looking for gold it is more important to look for light because, in a manner of speaking, light represents the head and gold represents the tail. Light is the soul and gold is the body. If you touch the body without touching the soul, you actually touch nothing. If you possess the body without possessing the soul, all you have is a corpse. You should also understand that it is dangerous to want to possess gold before possessing light. You know what happens when you pick up a snake by its tail: you get bitten. You should pick up a snake by its head, and you will not only be safe, but the tail will then follow the head.

July 4

We always hear the praises being sung of 'scientific truth'. Far more important than scientific truth, however, is the truth of life. The truth of life is learning to situate all forms of life within the cosmic structure in order to see how they vibrate in harmony and how they participate in the life of the Whole.

It is therefore not sufficient to observe and study all the elements of nature in fine detail; you must go further and see how they are connected, understand how that indefinable 'something', that none of them have independently of each other, circulates from one to the other: that 'something' which is life. True knowledge and understanding is found in life. As soon as you separate the various elements, life is no longer present. The quintessence of a certain mineral or plant is not revealed through knowledge of its make-up, smell, taste or colour, because if you look at anything in isolation you cut it off from life. Unite anything with all the other elements of earth and sky, then life becomes apparent, and true knowledge and understanding is yours.

Watch a person of a very tender age: the slightest incident gives rise to dramatic scenes of distress, upheaval and outbursts of all kinds. That is why his divine Self cannot yet flourish in him. As the years go by, however, he gradually settles down, calm starts to take hold, silence establishes itself within, and all his qualities start to appear. Previously, these same qualities remained hidden, unable to manifest because conditions were not right.

Observe vegetation in nature; occasionally some plants grow prematurely before the winter is out, and if there is the misfortune of a storm or a heavy frost, they uproot or freeze to death. A plant cannot really flourish as long as conditions are not favourable. Well, the same is true with people: as long as they are exposed to storms or extreme temperatures they cannot hear the inner voice of wisdom, the voice of the higher Self. Passions must first calm down, and only this calm provides the right conditions for all the good qualities to show themselves.

The clairvoyance of mediums is more or less always limited to the astral plane[1]. When you ask a medium to reach far distant regions to answer questions of a spiritual or cosmic nature, most of the time he or she is not able to. This kind of clairvoyance holds no interest for initiates because it cannot help people to become conscious of higher states. That is why initiates do not choose to linger on the astral plane: in fact, they even keep their eyes tightly closed as they cross these astral regions.

A true initiate does not seek to develop mediumistic powers. He only works on purifying himself, on developing wisdom, love and self-control in order to reach the summit. And once he has reached the summit, the substance of his being has become so pure that it is impregnated with the very quintessence of the universal Soul. This quintessence, on which everything is recorded, gives him the ability to see and sense all he wishes to know. That is how, through his work, he not only acquires power, but also achieves true clairvoyance.

---

[1] See note and diagram pages 366-367

All human adventure is basically the search for a lost half. Men seek out women and women seek out men. They do not even know why they seek each other out, but they do, instinctively: a voice tells them that that is how they will find their primordial integrity again. From time to time, for a few minutes or a few seconds, they taste something of an indescribable happiness, a mysterious dilation, but it does not last and then, inevitably, disappointment and sorrow follow. Since, however, they never lose hope, they continue their search. And why? Why are human beings unable to make their deepest aspirations come true? Because it is not on the physical plane that this union should first take place. The physical plane should only be the outcome of work previously completed on the mental, emotional and spiritual planes. Otherwise all they will find, at best, is momentary pleasure and enjoyment. In very rare instances it has happened that some have succeeded in achieving this unity on the physical plane for a length of time, and this is because they had previously embarked on substantial work on their inner selves. Every human being must first seek to unite the two principles within himself. That is the philosophy of the androgyne, and that is the highest philosophy there is.

July 8

Some young people, captivated by adventure, want to travel to faraway countries to live amongst the indigenous population because, they say, they feel restricted, undermined and let down by western society, the 'consumer' society.

What is their true objective, however? Do they really want to care for people, help them to feed themselves, and teach them? Or are they just looking for adventure? In the first case this experience could be interesting, useful and beneficial, both for them and for others. In the second instance, however, they will do no good to others, and they themselves will gain nothing since their objective is not a disinterested one – in fact quite the contrary – so they will return impoverished and disappointed. In reality very few people are able to reach a deep understanding of peoples with a very different mentality from theirs, and so bring them effective aid. We can make ourselves useful wherever we are – we do not have to go to the other end of the world.

Many people refuse to admit that they can resolve their problems with the very simple methods given to them by sages, because they feel that these methods are too simple. They demand cabbalistic formulas and displays of magic tricks. If, in order to free them from their troubles, a sage, an initiate, tells them: 'Close your eyes, calm yourself, breathe, send your love to the whole of humanity, to the whole of nature, bring yourself in harmony with the universe,' they do not listen. Instead of using these methods, and thus discovering their true value, they will go and seek out bogus magi to ask for a talisman or for revelations of the secrets of the ancient Tibetans or Aztecs. And then they find that the talisman or the secrets are totally ineffective. In order to achieve major results and acquire great spiritual riches you must have deep respect for methods and rules which may appear insignificant but which are, in fact, highly effective, because they are based on an extensive knowledge of human nature.

When we undertake 'spiritual work', we work on our inner self. From the moment we decide to undertake this work we undergo, without being aware of it, a gradual process of separation from ourselves, and as we continue this work we become progressively more aware of this separation. We increasingly see the difference between the part that does the work – the spirit, and that which is the object – the substance that is worked on. We even end up realizing that the thoughts and feelings, with which we do this work, are only instruments there for our benefit; and we understand that our true self lies beyond thoughts, feelings and actions.

To distance yourself from yourself, however, does not mean that you should leave yourself permanently. We do not abandon this self from which we distance ourselves, quite the contrary: we keep it well in sight, and once we have elevated ourselves to heaven through thought, we come back down in order to give it better direction, and refine its substance. Then again we distance ourselves and again we draw closer, and each time we bring it more strength and more light.

Whatever you do, be aware that there is always a force that pushes you forward, and another which watches you and lays its plans. When you do good, it is because you have been impelled forward by good, but evil is watching you, also waiting for the right moment to manifest itself. Furthermore, if you want to go further than is necessary be aware that evil will gnaw away at the excess – and will sometimes even swallow up the lot. That is why you should know restraint, even when it comes to doing good, otherwise you are in danger of triggering adverse forces. Why do people say that 'best is the enemy of good'? Because if you overdo good, you provoke evil.

Take heart, however, because when you do evil, good is watching you too, and is looking for a way to save you. If you are honest and sincere, even the mistakes you make will, one day, end up being put down to experience: experience which will have contributed to your spiritual growth.

One fine summer's evening some country folk were dancing on the village square merrily stamping the ground with the heels of their boots. A young farm labourer, who was extremely poor, stood watching, since he had no boots and therefore could not join in the dancing. He so wanted to join in that he asked his friend to lend him his boots. Happy that he could finally join the circle of dancers, he started to stamp his feet vigorously. On seeing this, his friend shouted: 'Hey, don't stamp your feet so hard, you'll ruin my boots!' The young man came away feeling deeply embarrassed that everyone now knew that he had had to borrow the boots. Another friend, seeing his embarrassment, said to him quietly: 'Take off those boots, I'll lend you some with which you can dance however you please.' The young man changed boots and rejoined the dancers. Having just taken his first steps in the dance his friend called out: 'Go on! Stamp as hard as you like, if you ruin those boots I'll lend you another pair.' Once again the young man blushed with embarrassment, because for the second time, everyone heard that he had no boots of his own.

Like the young man's two friends, people's lower nature makes itself heard by shouting about the services rendered. Good deeds must be secret. Jesus said: 'Do not let your left hand know what your right is doing,' in other words, do not let your lower nature know what your higher nature is doing, because otherwise your lower nature will boast about it and ruin everything.

One of the greatest sources of sorrow to men and women is that of having no children to take their place when they are no longer around. In the past, a family that did not have children was not appreciated by others. Read the Old Testament, which states that the greatest joy a father and mother have, even at the time of death, is the thought that they are leaving behind noble and intelligent children. They are proud of their children and, when they are on the other side, they find comfort in thinking they have left descendants. It is the same for a tree: a tree's greatest sorrow is not to bear fruit. All trees that are not fruit trees are at an inferior level in the evolutionary process. If you want to please a tree, say to it: 'My dear tree, I wish you the very best with all my heart and hope that one day you may become a fruit tree.' The tree will quiver with joy, because what it wants most in life is to become a fruit tree. And the same goes for a spiritual master, indeed to an even greater degree. The greatest joy for a master is to have good and intelligent disciples, with whom he will be able to go before the Great White Brotherhood up above and say: 'These are my sons and daughters.'

On a clear evening, stop a moment and gaze up at the stars. Imagine that you are leaving the earth behind with its conflicts and tragic events and that you become a citizen of the skies. Meditate on the beauty of the constellations and the immensity of the beings which inhabit them. As you rise up into space, you will feel yourself become lighter and freer, but you will above all find peace, a peace that will gradually seep into all the cells of your being. By meditating on the Wisdom that created the universe and the creatures that inhabit it, you will feel your soul putting out very subtle antennae, which allow it to communicate with the most distantly remote regions. Those are sublime moments which you will never forget.

It is not enough to want to correct your faults, you have to know how to go about correcting them. If you are forever struggling against your bad habits and inclinations, finding them difficult to shake off, you will end up discouraged and unhappy. So, instead of pondering over your weaknesses and failures, which are the result of bad habits acquired in the past, it is far better to focus on what you must do in the future and tell yourself: 'I shall put everything right, change everything for the better,' and work along those lines every day and with unwavering faith. In other words, take all the elements that God has given you, imagination, thought and feeling, and concentrate on conjuring up within yourself the most beautiful images: seeing yourself surrounded by music, seeing yourself in the light, seeing yourself in the sun, with the most perfect form, with qualities, talents and virtues – goodness, generosity, the ability to support others, help and enlighten them. Since everything is recorded, get into the habit of recording all that is best. Once you start on this work it will provide you with an infinite source of inspiration because you will be building the temple of the Divine within you.

The spirits of nature like being given work, but they never concern themselves about the objective of this work, be it good or evil, beneficial or detrimental. Whoever it may be who gives them the work, they do it: they are in total submission to this superior will that has succeeded in dominating them. That is why so many magicians and sorcerers use them for abhorrent purposes. The spirits of nature obey, because that is how they are: they have no moral conscience, they do everything, whether good or evil, in the same way. Knowing this, it is up to human beings to be vigilant and to learn to use these nature spirits only for divine work.

Ask this multitude of spirits, who are busily active in contributing to the life of nature, to give their assistance to all those who work for love, light and peace, for the coming of the Kingdom of God on earth.

From the initiatic point of view success is not always desirable. Obviously, if a person is weak and sickly it is best that he does not encounter too many major obstacles on his way, because if he falls down he will never get up again. If he is strong, however, setbacks and failure will strengthen him further: misfortune and enemies will give him energy, as if they were food for him, making him become, one day, invincible.

Unfortunately there are not many people who pursue their course with courage, despite the obstacles and misfortune they encounter. Most are easily discouraged and overwhelmed. You need to have gone a long way along the road of personal growth to draw strength from misfortune. Sometimes even heaven sets trials for certain people because it knows their nature, that they need to be faced with the greatest difficulties to help them reach the summit. Whereas others are spared because heaven knows that they would soon end up in trouble. Heaven therefore adapts its actions to each individual. That is why it is difficult to foretell human beings' destiny. Often misfortunes seem to be a punishment sent down from heaven whereas the opposite is true: they are the right conditions to oblige people to climb to the top.

When you are not used to observing and thoroughly studying the slightest details of everyday life, you do not see what people's behaviour reveals. Someone acts or moves in a surprising or even disturbing way, and it is generally thought to be an accident, or coincidence, or that this person had been subjected to the influence of something, or someone. The truth is that this person started to infringe the laws a long time before and it is only now that the results are showing. A gesture is never isolated. A gesture is the outcome of an entire story that shows how this person has grown, how he has lived, what he has felt, how he has acted. To anyone who is able to situate it correctly and link it to a whole, a gesture is the reflection of an entire world, the consequence of a whole train of former thoughts, feelings and actions. As long as human beings continually refuse to see the connection between things they will never be good psychologists.

There was once an old woman who always put some money aside in case she should be robbed. A thief obviously did come one day and the woman said: ‘Ah, there you are, I’ve been waiting for you. I have put something aside for you.’ The thief was totally amazed, but left very happy. The woman did not realize that by putting money aside she actually attracted the thief. Perhaps not many people are like this woman, but there are many who put money aside ‘for a rainy day’. Well, in doing so they attract the ‘rainy days’. It is magic, truly, it is unconscious black magic. You should never save up for a rainy day because, by doing so, you attract them. Save for a ‘sunny day’ so that when your princess finally comes you will be able to say: ‘I have the money to marry her’. Obviously the princess is symbolic: this princess is in fact all the happy events that occur in life.

Some spiritual teachings advise their followers to empty themselves, claiming that in this receptive and passive state they will receive the divine presence. This is a dangerous method which we do not advocate. When you are passive there is no certainty that what you receive will be the Divinity: rather, it will be negative entities from the invisible world which, seeing a man so weak and unprotected, are delighted to find a place in which to settle.

If you empty yourself without first having set in motion the active principle, which will set about working to clean and purify, you are at the mercy of the worst of entities. People empty themselves thinking that the holy Spirit will come. Yes, it is true, someone will come, but not the holy Spirit: it will be devils. The holy Spirit does not come to a swamp, he comes to a place that has been purified and illuminated for Him.

If you focus your attention on the visible, material world, you limit yourself, you become impoverished, and you become more material, too. Whereas if you focus on the inner world, the spiritual world, you will feel that everything you are living which is pure and luminous is uniting you with other beings, and other energies, right to infinity. The spiritual world represents riches and immensity, and if you work with it, you unite yourself with all the creative forces, with all the luminous entities which circulate across the stars and the constellations, to all the worlds in the universe; and you will taste divine life.

If you are but a small flame, the slightest breath of air will blow you out. If on the other hand you are a blazing fire, the stronger the wind the more your fire will spread. Yes, as long as you stay small, weak and sickly, as long as you are not yet firm and strong, the slightest obstacle will bring you down. Whereas if you are solid and strong all the difficulties you encounter will only strengthen your drive and enthusiasm, your will and your love. It happens all the time. At the slightest opposition the weak become discouraged and give up, whilst the strong become fired with even more determination to continue and fight the obstacles that confront them. So, do not ask me any more at what stage you are – you can find out for yourself: if you are stumped by the slightest problem in your life, you are still only a small candle.

We are living creatures, and to keep alive all living creatures must receive elements from creation – food, water, air, sun, etc. – and use all the riches matter can provide. Only the Creator defies this law: He does not need anything outside Himself. Since, however, he has left something of Himself in every living creature – a spark, a spirit that is of the same nature as Himself – each individual also has the potential to become a creator. Instead of always waiting for everything to come from outside us, we can act on the inside by means of our thought and will, and thus capture the greatest number of elements we need to feed ourselves physically, mentally, emotionally and spiritually. That is why the teachings of the initiates have always been the teachings of the creator spirit and, if you accept these teachings, you will always be strong, free, and rise high over all circumstances.

Every element, every object, every situation, and every living creature is a source of energy: but for this energy to manifest itself it has to be moved into a state of unbalance, in other words, on to an incline. Look at water, for instance: when water is put on a flat surface it spreads and turns into a still pool. Put this water on a steep incline and it will sweep away everything in its path.

The same applies to people. There is an incline in every person down which forces ceaselessly cascade, and these forces must be channelled to ensure they produce good work. However, this incline must constantly be re-balanced, because overload at one end produces a reaction of overload at the other. We see this, for instance, with people who are overexcited one moment and cast down the next. Our mental, emotional and spiritual life is based on a certain unbalance and this unbalance, if controlled, brings riches and creativity. Geniuses, for example, are not balanced people in the ordinary sense of the word – balance in the sense of 'ordinary' often only generates mediocrity. In fact, the opposite is true: geniuses are often people who, feeling threatened by dark forces, try to keep them in control by means of work and creativity. That is how they achieve great works.

Bees draw nectar from flowers and make it into a delicious food: honey. This symbolizes, also, the work of the initiate or the advanced disciple. Just as a bee draws the nectar from flowers without ever damaging them, the initiate only draws close to people to collect their most spiritual quintessence, and thanks to his knowledge of alchemy, he prepares in his heart and soul a nourishment of such delicious taste and smell the angels delight to savour it. That is what a bee is – an initiate: he always manages to find a divine quintessence in every human soul – even in those who have fallen very low – and with all this harvested quintessence he makes honey which is the food of celestial entities.

All problems can be resolved, provided we know human beings well – their structure, their inner strengths, and their relationship with the universe – according to the methods of esoteric science, which has been studying this matter over thousands of years. Many scientists and scholars think of man as a machine, some even insist on comparing man to a clockwork mechanism. These scientists and scholars do not realize that man has unknown and, as yet, undiscovered powers – entities and intelligences – within him, which are capable, given the right conditions, of creating elements in the organism which were not present before. They do not realize that, as well as a physical body, man also has other bodies of a more subtle nature: the etheric, astral, mental, causal, buddhic and atmic bodies[1]. They do not fully know what the intellect, the heart and the will are, and even less so the soul and spirit. And they imagine that they can cure people? Impossible! It is impossible because they go about it in the wrong way: they do not want to understand what a human being really is.

---

[1] See note and diagram pages 366-367

Watch yourself, and you will find that you are always ready to follow the advice of your lower nature. When it tells you: 'Look at him, he cheated on you, he has hurt you, you should teach him a lesson!' you rush to obey your lower nature, thinking you are right and that justice is on your side. Well, you are mistaken, and from now on you must make sure that you are able to analyze where every impulse comes from. You will find that, more often than not, it is your lower self that is advising you and, if so, you must realize that the end result will always be bad.

It takes years to acquire this skill of discernment – it is not easy. Indeed it is very tenuous, because the lower nature can take on so many different guises, so many deceptive voices and appearances. Hence, a true initiate is a person who has practised all his life to differentiate between the impulses originating from his lower self, and those which come from his higher Self. 'Is that all?' I hear you say. Yes, everything depends on this ability to differentiate, this all-important skill of discernment. As long as you do not work at acquiring this skill, you will be weak, sickly and unhappy.

We take everything we need for our existence from nature: even when we manufacture products, we have to use the materials we find in nature. Nature, however, is not there to satisfy the appetite and whims of human beings. If people continue to exploit nature without consideration, if they continue to pollute and plunder, first they will destroy themselves. Then, once nature has rid herself of human beings by wiping them off the face of the earth, she will regain the upper hand. Nature has resources; she does not allow herself to be vanquished so easily. If human beings do not strive to live and work in harmony with nature, nature will defend herself and may even, finally, eradicate them.

Since women are closer to matter they are more realistic, more down-to-earth and practical, with more good common sense. Whereas men, who are more at ease in the sphere of thought and abstraction, tend to lose themselves in theories that end up bearing little relation to the realities of everyday life.

Women's behaviour and attitude are linked to their capacity for being a mother, and even if they do not have children they have maternal qualities such as devotion, compassion and concern for others less strong than themselves, and for all living creatures. Consider this: how long does it take the man to play his part in creating a child? A few moments, and he is then able, if he so wishes, to concern himself no longer with the matter, to forget about the fact that he has made a child: in fact, he may never even know. As for the woman, how could she not know, or how could she ever forget that she carries or has given birth to a child? And when this child is born, how could she fail to look after this tiny delicate creature? Whereas, often, the man has already departed elsewhere. Whether we like it or not, the role that men and women each play in this truly fundamental act of perpetuating life greatly affects their temperament and their way of looking at things.

If you want to win someone's love or friendship, never exert pressure on them by means of money, gifts, seduction, or bribery. Everyone else uses these methods as they are successful and easy: but do not use them yourselves. The only method you have the right to use is light: it is the only truly effective method. Send gifts of spiritual light to those whose love you would like to win, and spread that light all around them. When you want someone to love you, to think of you, send him light: his soul, which will feel the presence of a beneficial entity, will appreciate you more and more.

In order to keep the sacred inner fire alight, you must feed it pieces of your lower nature every day. Yes, because it is the lower nature, the personality, that is predestined to feed the fire of the spirit. Stop questioning the use of your lower nature and wondering how you can rid yourself of it: without it, not only would survival on earth be impossible, but you would have nothing with which to feed your spirit.

Know that a magical law exists, according to which results on the divine plane can only be obtained if you sacrifice something of your personality. And if you go and find an initiate, a magus, or a great master to ask him to cure you, a member of your family, or a friend, or ensure the success of some enterprise, or another such request, he will tell you that the only possible way to do so is to renounce certain weaknesses and harmful habits. When you abstain from indulging in mediocre pleasures, an energy is released, which feeds your ability to realize all the good you desire, both for yourselves and for others.

When a child is small the only things that matter to him are feeding himself, and playing with everything around him, and as soon as he is denied the slightest thing, he screams and yells. Children are little monsters of selfishness, but at that age it is normal. Adults, the father and the mother, understand they can expect nothing else. If, however, the child continues to behave in the same way when he is older, he is reprimanded, or maybe even smacked, because he needs to change and stop thinking only of himself. Later on he will need to couple with a partner and, subsequently, have children. Why has cosmic intelligence arranged things in this way? To persuade people to look after others, rather than themselves alone: and the first step is to care for a husband, or wife, and children. Cosmic intelligence wants to teach this lesson, but how many people have understood it? How many people are capable of forgetting their own self-interest a little, and thinking about their husband, their wife and their children in a sincerely unselfish way?

Too many people live any old how the entire day, and then in the evening, before going to sleep, they say a little prayer to ask God to forgive them their wrong-doings. Well, it is not enough: these people should know that this behaviour is certain to keep the devil always at their side, like the monk in this story:

'There was once a kindly monk, who drank and drank. Every day the level of the wine in the barrels went down visibly. Somewhat shamefacedly, of course, he said his prayers every night and asked God for forgiveness, after which, his mind at rest, he slept peacefully until the following day, when he started all over again. This went on for years. One evening, however, he forgot to say his prayers, and during the night he suddenly felt someone shake him, saying: 'Hey, you didn't say your prayers tonight. Get up at once and say your prayers!' He woke up, rubbed his eyes and what did he see? The devil! Yes, it was the devil who had woken him; it was he who made the monk say his prayers every night. And why? To stop the monk from mending his ways. Since the monk said his prayers by asking God for forgiveness, his conscience was clear and the following day he would start drinking all over again, to the great joy of the devil. When the monk understood this he was so alarmed he gave up drinking once and for all.

People who meditate on the geometry of crystals and precious stones to understand their structures come close to true science – the science of principles. And one day, they will be able to visit the bowels of the earth and see how the spirits of nature work on the minerals. They will visit the sites where billions of intelligent entities work their hardest to reproduce on earth the beauty and perfection of heaven.

In reality no precious stone, however precious it may be, will ever succeed in being an exact reflection of heaven, the beauty of which has no equal. The physical plane is far from being comparable to heaven, but it can at least sometimes give us an image of it. Flowers, precious stones, etc. are also a reflection of the divine world: in their unique way, they remind us of the purity, transparency, lucidity and perfection of heaven.

Whatever the mental and material conditions in which you find yourself, never let yourself be weakened by the thought that evil, in all its forms, could easily befall you. If you always feel weak and vulnerable and without protection, then, yes, you really are exposed. Work with thought to unite with celestial entities, and with light; lead an honest and pure life, and you will be protected. Admittedly, there will be people who will try to harm you with black magic, but it will all fall back on to them, because of the boomerang effect of the law of return shock. Evil cannot enter a person who is occupied by the Lord and taken over by angels: in such a person, evil is immediately rejected, and returns to the person who sent it in the first place. Cling on to that idea, and already you will be out of harm's way.

Do you know this story written by Tolstoy? One day a king picked up a seed that was the size of a nut. He called upon the knowledge of all the sages at his court, but none was able to tell him where the seed came from. However, he was told of a very old man who lived in his kingdom, who might be able to help. The king sent for the man who arrived supported by two crutches and was nearly blind. The old man examined the seed for a long time and finally said: 'Your Majesty, I do not know what this giant seed is, but if you will allow me, I shall fetch my father who may remember having seen a similar one.' The father arrived, supported by one single crutch. He was not able to identify the seed either, but he suggested calling upon his father. The latter soon arrived; he looked like a young man, strong and in good spirits. He took hold of the seed and cried out: 'But this is a grain of wheat that used to grow when I was a child. At that time wheat had very large grains, but since people started to harm each other, steal from each other and massacre each other, the grains of wheat have become smaller and smaller. And if I look so strong and younger than my son and grandson, it is because I continue to live by the rules of honesty and goodness that governed life when I was a child.'

If you have people near you who are difficult to bear, it is to teach you to love. One day, when you leave earth and you stand before the celestial entities, they will ask you to account for what you have done on earth:
– 'Why did you not love your fellow-creatures?
– 'Well, because they were nasty, stupid, and selfish.'
– 'No, that is not a reason. Heaven gave you great riches: you were given eyes, a mouth, ears, arms and legs, and you were given these to love, and not to spread slander, despise, create havoc, and ride roughshod over everyone and everything.'
– 'But they were so awful!'
– 'All the more reason to be increasingly generous.'

There are no excuses to justify your actions.

The heart and the intellect are useful; they are necessary, but they are not enough for a true understanding of life without a third faculty, intuition, which is both an understanding and a feeling. Be careful, however, not to confuse intuition with clairvoyance. Intuition is superior to clairvoyance. Clairvoyance is a faculty that only allows you to look objectively at the astral and the mental plane[1]. You can be clairvoyant and not understand anything you are seeing. Whereas with intuition you may not see anything, but you understand things as if you saw them one hundred per cent more clearly, because you are living and experiencing them.

---

1 See note and diagram pages 366-367

August 11

It is vital to know how to gauge the measure in all things. Yes, even in goodness, because if you know no bounds in this either, you will inevitably suffer the consequences. Not knowing how to gauge the correct measure is neither a crime nor wickedness, but it is a fault, and all faults have unfortunate consequences.

Let me give you an example. A woman came to see me and said:

– 'Oh Master, I am so unhappy. I can't stop crying.'

– 'But why? What has happened?'

– 'Well, I, who have loved my husband so dearly, who have done everything for him, who have anticipated all his wishes and have always showed him a great deal of affection and warmth, well, I have been left in the lurch by him; he has gone off with one of my friends.'

– 'And what is this friend like?'

– 'Well, she is selfish and cold.'

– 'That is exactly what the problem is; you are too warm, he has gone to refresh himself.':

– ' So goodness is useless?' I can already hear you say.

Unfortunately stupid goodness can lead someone into the worst of situations. Even the most marvellous people get hit on the head if they know no bounds. It is not a punishment: but through their ignorance they have set a law in motion, and they suffer the backlash.

Some call the sun 'the lamp of the universe', to express the idea that the sun illuminates the world and, thanks to its light, we are able to see. And when it is not the sun providing light, we need another source: an electric light bulb, candles, a torch, head-lights, etc. Objects are only visible to the extent that light falls on them and illuminates them: that is a law of the physical world and it is also a law of the spiritual world. However, there are no lamps in the spiritual world that we can light in the way that we turn on the light in our bedroom or on the stairs: if we want to see, we ourselves have to project light. So few people are able to see on the spiritual plane, because they wait for objects to be illuminated, whereas it is up to them to project the rays of light that will allow them to see.

Physicists teach us that every particle of matter has an energy. This energy is a masculine principle, and matter is a feminine principle. Our physical body, which consists of matter, also has an energy, and it is this energy we call the soul. However, in reality, man is made up of several bodies[1] and each body has a soul. For the physical body it is the instinctive soul; for the astral body the emotional soul; and for the mental body it is the intellectual soul. And the causal, buddhic and atmic bodies also each have a soul. Each body has a soul: the body is the container and the soul is the content – the two are linked. Nature herself, the cosmos, is a body, which is the body of God, and it has a soul: the universal Soul which fills the cosmos. All this is really very clear and straightforward. Humans have complicated matters because they lack knowledge, but in initiatic science it is simple: there are as many souls as there are bodies.

1 See note and diagram pages 366-367

The soul needs space: it needs immensity in order to breathe, dilate and rejoice. Limit this space and the soul is suffocated, wilts, and wastes away. And that is what happens to people who concentrate on all the material details of everyday life without ever taking a moment to immerse themselves in immensity, and find fulfilment.

It goes without saying that, in some cases, limitation is necessary. The birth of a child, for instance, is nothing but a limitation, but it is a necessary limitation in order for this manifestation to happen. The human being who comes down to incarnate into matter must limit himself. At the time of death, however, he will return toward immensity. Life is made up of these two processes: limitation and dilation, and to be happy you must be able to apply them both to your daily lives. You enter into your conscience to unite with the universe, with the universal Soul, then you return to a state of limitation to work. Do not stay in this limited state too long, however, because if you do, you will become bored and will suffer. Think about setting out again on the road of immensity soon.

The one vital thing that a master wants to give to his disciples is the light of initiatic science, because he knows that once they have this light they will be able to face all problems and, even, no longer need his presence. In order to help people they must be given a spiritual element which becomes part of them. Many people do not realize this. When they want to do good they give something material, instead of remembering that they can give this spiritual element, which will never fade away. They are still ignorant of what is essential, so they give money, food and medicines. I am not saying that these are not useful, but if you want to give the quintessence, you must learn to give light.

The need to dominate, to have power, is so strong in some people that we now see the most materialistic scientists starting to explore the field of initiatic science – telepathy, clairvoyance, clairaudience, radiesthesia and psychometry – and they classify all this as 'parapsychology'. Providing it can give them power over others they will accept any theory, however insane they may have found it previously. They accept any knowledge of initiatic science which can help them achieve their aims, and they reject any knowledge which cannot give them power. However, using initiatic truths as a means to dominate others is highly immoral, and those who do so will be punished by heaven. You should only use this spiritual knowledge to help and comfort others, to spread light and peace in the world. Then it will be noted in heaven that you are a white magus, and soon divine blessings will start to rain down upon you.

How many times have you heard people say: 'I am so tired!' Very few people really know what tiredness is. Tiredness is something that clings to you, just as some clinging women won’t let go of their men, always demanding to be loved and kept company. Because people accept tiredness and are preoccupied by it, they reinforce their fatigue so it keeps coming back, and is always there.

So, try to change your attitude and you will see what happens. Let us say, for instance, that every morning as you wake up you think: 'Oh, I'm so tired, I don't want to see the sunrise,' and you go back to sleep. Finally, one day you say: 'Yes, it's true, I don't feel like getting up, but I want things to change. I’ll get up, anyway.' So up you get, you wash your face and go out into the fresh air, and suddenly you no longer feel tired: tiredness has left you. If you want tiredness to leave you, you must do something about it. If you do nothing to counter tiredness, it will never leave you.

As long as you do not have a truly spiritual ideal the forces and energies you carry within you will not be mobilized in the same direction, and the whole of your life will be disorganized. Look at the life most people lead: what a mess, what chaos! Some people do have an ideal, but in the majority of cases it is to get rich, achieve glory and dominate others. In the eyes of God, however, that is not an ideal. Of course these people have a far more interesting life than those who content themselves with modest ambitions. You can write books and make films about their lives. Yes, and what fascinating stories they make: how they cheated and got the better of a rival, how they ruined a competitor. Sooner or later, however, heaven will punish them for using their talents to satisfy all their lower tendencies instead of devoting them to making a divine ideal come true.

Sometimes you complain that you have been watching the sunrise for twenty years and feel no benefit, and that no divine seeds are growing within you. Twenty years is not very long. Some of the seeds deep within you need centuries, or even millennia, to grow.

Some planets, like Mercury, Venus and the Moon have a fast revolution and their influence is short and superficial, while others like Jupiter, Saturn, Uranus and Pluto have a slower revolution, and that is why their influence is deeper and more tangible. Some things, therefore, you can achieve quickly: you can have a job, a house, a wife or husband and children within a few years. However, learning to be reasonable, patient, in control of oneself, or generous, takes a very long time, because the 'orbits' of these qualities are vast. That is why you must continue to warm yourself in the rays of the spiritual sun and then, one fine day, everything will grow. Never doubt the effectiveness of the sun in your spiritual life.

It is said that it is the Church – the clergy – who invented morals in order to dominate and exploit the credulous and ignorant populace. It is true that, in many cases, the clergy used religion in the zealous service of totally shameful purposes. However, true religion, true morals, are based on a science, the science of causes and consequences, and not on some personal interest. Every thought, every feeling, every action has positive and negative consequences for people. Where the clergy went wrong was that they did not try to explain the rules they imposed. People were told: 'Do this … do that …,' like children who are asked to obey, without any explanation. That is why, like children, everybody disobeyed at the first opportunity, whereas people should have been informed that true religion, like true morality, is based on a knowledge of the great cosmic laws. This knowledge would have helped their evolution.

Get into the habit of talking to the flowers, the birds, the trees, the animals and people with love, because it is a divine habit. People who can say words that warm, inspire and light up the sacred fire, use the magic wand in their mouths.

Always be attentive to your thoughts and words, because in nature one of the four elements – earth, water, air or fire – is always there, waiting for the opportunity to create matter from everything you think and say. This is an infallible law, although it often has consequences far removed from the person who first gave nature the seeds. Just as the wind sweeps up seeds and sows them far away, so your thoughts and words fly away and end up somewhere in space producing results, either good or bad.

There are several ways to penetrate the spiritual world. Meditation, together with prayer, is one of the most accessible. Meditation, however, implies preparation. If you start to meditate without having first achieved an internal discipline, in other words having achieved control over your thoughts, your feelings and your desires, you will err into the lower regions of the astral plane[1], disturbing layers of darkness inhabited by entities who are often hostile to human beings. That is how you fall prey to hallucinations bearing no relation to the object of your meditation. Before meditating you should therefore start by putting your mental, emotional and psychic being in order, otherwise even an exercise as useful and beneficial as meditation can become dangerous.

---

1 See note and diagram pages 366-367

Physically a person can only be a man or a woman, and generally speaking it is impossible to be mistaken on this point. Psychically, however, things are far more complex. Psychically a person has the two principles: the masculine and the feminine. Man can therefore not be likened to the masculine principle, nor woman to the feminine principle. In the Chinese representation of yin and yang, for instance, the black, feminine yin contains a white dot, and the white, masculine yang contains a black dot, to explain that the masculine always contains a feminine part and the feminine always contains a part which is masculine.

Living men and women are not abstract principles: living men and women are a combination of masculine and feminine in unequal proportions and, what is more, from one incarnation to another they may even change sex physically. It has been established by cosmic intelligence that, in order to grow and perfect their inner self, people should know the two states, the two conditions, and so learn to acquire all the qualities of both principles.

Even if you are not aware of it, everything around you influences you, and this is the most important point of all. You must become aware of this fact so you can work correctly on your personal growth. As soon as you sense that a creature, an object, or a natural phenomenon has a favourable effect on you, make a conscious effort to open your inner doors to allow these influences to penetrate deep within you. If you do not allow yourself to open up to good influences, even the most beneficial things will remain useless.

Go to a spring or a fountain and imagine that it flows through you. Go to the sun, watch it, open yourself up to it, so that it may awaken all the warmth and light of your inner spiritual sun. Go to the flowers and ask them the secret of their colour and their scent, and listen to them so that you, too, may learn to extract the most deliciously perfumed quintessence from your heart and soul.

When a society makes its economic interests its prime concern, even when this society achieves major successes, the day will inevitably come when it is faced with problems that it did not have the wisdom to foresee. Here is an example: there is nothing more profitable for a country that manufactures arms than to export those arms. That is how increasingly murderous equipment is sold to peoples who, by fighting continuously, pose a threat to the peace and safety of the entire planet. Some of these peoples are barely able to read and write, but that does not stop arms dealers from supplying them with the most sophisticated weapons, even sending experts to train them in their use. On the one hand a great deal of money is made. That is true. On the other hand, however, these profits will have to be paid for dearly because there will be an inevitable result: huge problems, and the vast expenditure needed to put an end to the conflicts breaking out all over the world. We face insurmountable problems if we do not think things through and consider the end result. If immediate benefits are our sole concern, the problems will be even more serious.

Creation is the work of the number 2. What is this number 2, however? It is the number 1 polarized into positive and negative, masculine and feminine, active and passive. As soon as number 1 wants to manifest itself, it must divide. Unity is the privilege of God Himself, His exclusive domain. In order to create, God – the 1, had to become 2: there is no creation possible in 1 because there cannot be any exchange. God therefore projected Himself out of Himself by polarizing, and the universe was born from the existence of these two poles. The positive pole attracts the negative pole and the negative pole attracts the positive. It is this mechanism of action and reaction which sparks off and maintains the movement of life. Stopping this movement causes stagnation and death, the return to the initial indifferent state. The first lines of the Book of Genesis tell how creation occurred through a succession of divisions. On the first day of creation God separated light from darkness. On the second day He separated the waters above from the waters below. On the third day He gathered the waters of earth together. 1 is therefore an entity enclosed within itself. In order to be released, this entity must become 2.

A child who is always good and obedient will be considered ‘sweet and adorable’ by adults. A child who stays still when he is told to sit still, who is quiet when told to be quiet, is easier to cope with, of course, but what will become of this sweet, docile child later in life? Not a great deal: this child will remain insignificant. Whereas a child who is wilful and undisciplined, who causes trouble with his peers and whose parents, neighbours and educators endlessly complain is a terrible nuisance, who wears everyone down and upsets everyone, is precisely the child who is far more likely to become somebody outstanding. Today this child oversteps the limits, but tomorrow this child’s energies, personality and talent, once he has learned to channel them correctly, will lift him way above the rest. It is up to parents and educators to safeguard this development, to help the child achieve great things.

Purity alone allows intuition to develop. That is why, in our teaching, we attach such great importance to purity: living a pure life, eating pure food, drinking pure drink, breathing pure air, having pure thoughts and pure feelings.

Man's destiny depends on the clarity of his 'inner eye', and this clarity depends on his way of life. As soon as he commits an error and violates divine laws his spiritual vision clouds over, so he is no longer forewarned or guided, and he becomes entrenched in inextricable complications. Therefore, always try to become aware of the relationship that exists between your day-to-day behaviour and the clarity of your vision. If you decide to live a straight, honest and noble life, you purify yourself, and your subtle organs start to function. That is how, with proper guidance and direction, you will again find the springs, the fields, the lakes, the meadows and the mountains of your true homeland.

Nature is alive and intelligent. Yes, intelligent. It is not only human beings who possess the faculty of intelligence. Of course some find this difficult to admit, but they must realize that as our opinion of nature changes, so we change our destiny. Nature is the body of God. If we think it is dead and stupid we diminish life within us. On the other hand, if we think that nature is alive and intelligent, that stones, plants, animals and stars are also alive and intelligent, we also introduce life into ourselves. And since nature is alive and intelligent we must be extremely attentive towards it, and respectful of it, and look upon it with a feeling of sacredness.

What is the place of men and women? The day will come when men and women will have to sort out this problem, for it continuously goads them to find fault with one another. For centuries, or even millennia, men have imposed their dominance on women and now the reverse situation is beginning to become evident: women are standing up for themselves; they no longer accept to be dominated by men; they want the same rights as men and are even prepared to play the masculine role, usurping their position. There is nothing abnormal about this: it is the law of compensation in action. Men have gone too far. Instead of being paragons of honesty, goodness and righteousness, and so earning women's admiration and esteem, men have abused their authority and physical superiority over women. They have taken for themselves all the advantages and imposed only obligations on women. How could men ever think that this situation could last?

In reality, women do of course need to admire men, recognize their authority and their strength. But if men compromise themselves, how can women look up to this kind of superiority?

The palm tree is a tree that grows in the sands of the desert where the sun is fierce and water is scarce. The palm tree, however, says: 'This is what I can do in the worst of conditions,' and it produces dates, which are sweeter and more mellow than any other fruit. The palm tree is a true alchemist: it transmutes sand into sugar. On the other hand, another shrub planted in very rich soil, kept well watered and growing in a favourable climate, only manages to be a blackthorn, producing bitter fruits. Many people resemble the blackthorn: they live in favourable conditions but, even so, they bear bitter fruit, they are always complaining. This shows that they are not aware of the riches they possess within themselves, and do not know how they can make use of these riches. They should meditate on the image of the palm tree which flourishes and bears fruit in the worst conditions. That is why it is said in the Psalms: 'The righteous flourish like the palm tree.'

The disciple must develop his sensitivity. But this kind of sensitivity is far removed from that other, neurotic, morbid tendency to touchiness, which produces only upset and illness following the slightest criticism or most insignificant disagreement. Unfortunately everyone seems to harbour this kind of touchiness; it is all too common, and it is not true sensitivity. True sensitivity is an ability to perceive the presence of the invisible world, the energies that traverse space, and the entities which surround and visit us. In reality there is much more going on in the psychic world than in the physical world, and it is in the psychic world that you need to practise sensing energies, presences – everything that is intangible and subtle. True sensitivity is therefore sensitivity to the invisible world, but especially to all that is luminous and divine in the invisible world.

Food is of prime concern to people all over the world. Food is the problem that everyone seeks to resolve first and foremost: they work and even fight for it. This attitude towards food, however, is still only an impulse, an instinctive tendency that has not yet entered the sphere of enlightened consciousness. Only initiatic science teaches us that food, which is prepared with inexpressible wisdom in divine laboratories, contains magical elements capable of maintaining and restoring health, both physical, mental, emotional and spiritual health. But for this, we must examine the conditions in which these elements may be harnessed, and we must know that thought is the most effective of all means. Yes, indeed, because thought is capable of drawing out subtle, luminous particles from the food, particles which help build our whole being. In this way, little by little, we change.

When you come to understand nourishment it will become a source of goodness and wonder to you, because far beyond simply eating to stay alive, nourishment will begin to take on another significance, paving the way to other knowledge, other work to be done, other aims to be achieved. On the surface you will look as if you are eating like everyone else, and the entire world will be eating like you, but in reality there will be an immense difference, as great as between earth and heaven.

Two legs are better than one. You will probably say there is nothing new about that. So why are you still perched on one leg? Yes, I see you constantly hopping on one leg instead of walking: the sentimental among you on the left leg – they do not think; and the intellectuals on the right leg – their heart is completely dried up; all one-legged people. You see, you claim to be knowledgeable, but since you do not practise what you know, in fact you are ignorant.

Why does Mother Nature oblige people to walk in this way – first putting forward one foot, and then the other? The answer is simple: it is because people must act with their heart on some occasions and with their intellect on others, and they should know when to switch from one polarity to another. All the problems they encounter are caused by their failure to walk along using both legs.

If you are seeking an initiatic teaching solely to educate yourself and speed up your spiritual evolution, it is proof that your ideal is not so sublime: you are just looking to promote your self-interest, your own salvation. Too many people only think of the salvation of their soul. 'I want to save my soul!' they say. Well, that is not so wonderful. You should no longer be preoccupied with saving your soul. What do people think the soul is all about? What does one's soul represent compared with the immensity of creation as a whole? People should work at saving other people's souls, and then they themselves will also be saved. Otherwise, whilst they are busy worrying about saving their own souls, they isolate themselves from the rest of the world: nobody else matters to them, all they are thinking about is their own soul. It is neither sensible nor appealing. You must let that notion go. The day people rid themselves of the idea that they must always look after their own good, their personal salvation, the whole world will change, because this is the very idea which is preventing the coming of the Kingdom of God.

It is not on the physical plane that women are most powerful, but in the subtle plane of emanations, because they give off small, subtle particles of a special magnetism. That is why men have often called them witches, sorceresses, or fairies. The truth is that, thanks to their emanations, women even have the ability to form bodies of an etheric nature. If a great master, a saviour of the world, provides them with the seed, the idea, then all women are able to provide the material which serves to create the body of a collective child. They do, however, have to become conscious of their capabilities, and decide to contribute with the whole of their being to the formation and development of this new collective body: the Kingdom of God on earth.

Before undertaking any task make sure you are calm, and if it is a manual task, concentrate on the first movement and make that movement slowly, and make it correctly. Then repeat that same movement a little faster, and repeat it again and again until you have reached the required speed: you will see that the task will seem easier and easier, and at the same time be impeccably executed. This is the way you will be able to perform perfectly whatever task you are faced with.

If you make a mistake in any field today, it is because in the past, without realizing it, you had already laid the groundwork for this mistake. The first time you made some movement, or made contact with some object or person, you did it without care, without attaching importance to what you were doing, and now you are suffering the consequences. Mistakes accumulate and worsen as time goes by. Mistakes engraved upon us in the past are very difficult to make good in the present, but it is easy to learn to engrave correct, new habits.

It is important to think about the true meaning of scientific progress. Is the purpose of all these robots, these appliances, these machines and these means of transport simply to allow people to do nothing, to stop walking even, on the pretext that there are gadgets to do all that for them? No, all these improvements have come about to allow them to free themselves from the material activities which crush them, to allow them more time to devote themselves to spiritual, divine activities. That is the true meaning of technical progress: to free people to do other, more elevated work. Otherwise this progress could be very detrimental. If people have nothing more to do than stretch out on the grass or the sand somewhere, to stagnate and vegetate whilst machines do all the work, they will be ruined. It is important to understand that cosmic intelligence has permitted all this material progress to allow people to distance themselves from prosaic tasks, and devote themselves to sublime activities.

You often think: 'Why does the invisible world not give us prior warning of the trials we will have to endure?' Well, it is because, when we are faced with an unexpected situation, we are forced to go deeper within ourselves and make a greater effort. You will all have to face such trials – you will be glad to hear!

In the ancient initiations those who had to walk across fire were, in fact, really walking across an artificial fire, but they did not know that: they thought the fire was real. If they were frightened and drew back, it showed that they were not worthy of initiation, and so were sent away. Those, however, who were bold, daring, and full of faith, walked across the fire and subsequently discovered that it was only an illusion. You could say that all the trials of life are illusory. Before we tackle them, we think: 'How awful! I am going to suffer dreadfully.' But if we are able to handle them correctly, we must admit that, in reality, it was not so difficult after all.

Having descended to incarnate on the physical plane, human beings are so preoccupied with their external appearance as a man or as a woman they tend to forget that up above, on the divine plane, they possess both principles – masculine and feminine. You must understand, however, that 'up above' is not light years away. 'Up above' is also within us: it is the higher part of us. Women must understand that the masculine principle is there within them, waiting, and will reveal itself at the end of their spiritual quest by giving them strength, knowledge and wisdom. And in men the feminine principle is waiting within to give them true beauty, love, and divine life in all its abundance.

True initiation is an internal process at the end of which a human being is able to fuse with the complementary side of himself. That is why he never feels deprived or lonely. Men and women feel no less lonely if they have sexual relationships. Many people know that only too well. The number of their encounters and experiences increase, but inside the feeling of isolation, the solitude of the desert, persists. Yes, it is within, on the mental, emotional and spiritual planes, that certain encounters must first be made. You will only find below what you have first realized above.

You have to be able to transpose certain moral, philosophical or mystical notions on to a different plane. For instance, according to the Gospels, fasting drives out unclean spirits, but a fast should not only take place on the physical plane. If evil spirits are dwelling in the physical body in the form of illness, physical fasting may chase them away. However, these spirits may also be dwelling in the astral and mental body[1] in the form of irrational thoughts and coarse feelings and desires. If you are 'possessed', the spirits living within you will always urge you to absorb a nourishment pleasing to them. So, in order to rid yourself of these evil spirits do not give them anything more to eat: in other words, you should try not to have any more selfish feelings or self-centred thoughts, and replace them with pure, luminous thoughts and feelings. By depriving these dark spirits of their food you will make them fast and so, feeling the threat of death by starvation, they will leave you. That is how fasting should be understood.

---

1 See note and diagram pages 366-367

Cosmic intelligence has given every living creature a specific sound in order to participate in the universal symphony. Only human beings have the ability to cut themselves off from this symphony, because the Creator has given them free will. If they use this free will to give way to their instincts, their passions or their whims, they will distance themselves more and more from cosmic harmony and deprive themselves of its blessings. The day they decide to make unity and harmony their goal, their consciousness will expand: again they will vibrate in unison with the All, and will re-establish an inner conduit through which the purest energies of the universe will, once again, start to circulate and give them life.

Every day heaven speaks to us, sending us messages. However, these messages come from a sphere where matter is extremely subtle: they must pass through all the impure layers we have accumulated around us, and in the process they become deformed. Take a stick, put it in a container of water with transparent sides and look: at the precise point where it penetrates the water, the stick will seem to be broken. This deformation is due to the difference in density between water and air. The same applies on the psychic plane: the more things have to descend into the density of matter, the more they become deformed. In order to know them as they really are, you have to be able to elevate yourself through thought to the subtle world of their origin. A dense brain is not capable of receiving sublime truths from heaven. Or, rather, it receives them in a deformed state – the brain itself deforms them.

Seek therefore to clear away all impurities, to elevate yourself, and then – only then – will you receive clear, lucid and truthful answers from heaven.

Do you hate somebody? Well, be aware that hating someone is exactly the same as loving that person. You are creating a link between you both because hate is as powerful as love. If you want to free yourself from someone, do not hate him and do not love him either – be indifferent. If you hate a person, you tie yourself to that person with chains that no-one will be able to unfasten. You will always be tied together and the ties will remain for years, centuries even. Yes, you do not realize this. People imagine that by hating someone they distance themselves from the object of their hatred. Quite the contrary: hate is a force which ties you to the person you hate, and you will come across this person again in a following incarnation. Get this into your heads: hate forms ties that are as powerful as love. These ties are different, obviously: love will bring you certain things and hate will bring you others, but just as certainly and as powerfully as love.

The serpent is traditionally portrayed in two opposing ways: good and evil. In Genesis, Moses says that the serpent is 'the slyest of all beasts in the field'. It was the serpent who, as God's adversary, pushed Adam and Eve to disobey His orders. In the Book of Exodus, however, it is written that on the order of God, Moses had a serpent made out of bronze, and that whoever looked at this serpent would be healed. And when Jesus sends out his disciples he tells them: 'Be wary as serpents, innocent as doves.' He thus portrays the serpent as a symbol of wisdom. In India, too, sages are called 'nagui': serpents. What is the explanation for this apparent contradiction?

Since it was the serpent who pushed Adam and Eve to taste the fruit of the Tree of Knowledge of Good and Evil, we look upon it as a symbol of knowledge. Knowledge, however, is neutral. Whether it is good or evil depends on the way we use knowledge. The most educated people may be the greatest benefactors or the worst criminals. Knowledge empowers. Those who use it for evil purposes are united with the serpent of darkness: they are black magi. And those who use their knowledge for good purposes are united with the serpent of light: they are white magi.

The only way to liberate yourself is by becoming attached to something higher. Many people try to liberate themselves but they do so extremely clumsily, and even in a way that is dangerous to themselves and to others. Imagine that you have an old house you no longer want. Before destroying it you should build another, otherwise you will be out in the rain. In the same way you should become attached to something higher – a new way of thinking or living – before freeing yourself from everything which makes you suffer, or limits you. This attachment is like building a new house. Then you will be able to detach yourself: that is, demolish the old house by renouncing all that is negative and harmful. If you do the opposite, if you detach yourself before becoming attached, that detachment will not help: it may even be harmful because, having nothing more to cling to, you will be even more unhappy. You should not detach yourself before you are attached: you should not demolish before you have built.

It is generally believed that anything that is fine, delicate and tenuous is not as capable of withstanding aggression as something that is not. That is a mistake. Look at what happens in the different realms of nature. On the surface, stones would seem to be the toughest, but in reality plants are able to withstand more than stones because plants are also alive. And animals are able to withstand even more than plants because animals are able to move. And human beings have even more ways to escape difficult situations, but because they have not yet worked at refining and purifying themselves they continue to be at the mercy of circumstances, as well as of the forces and entities of the invisible world.

If you climb high up the ladder of beings you will find creatures which have so purified their bodies and so intensified their lives that they have become impossible to catch or restrict. And above all these creatures there is the Lord, who is the only being of such immateriality that He is totally elusive and indefinable: so much so, in fact, that we cannot even conceive of Him.

This love that men and women look for exclusively in one another is, in reality, to be found in the whole of nature, but in such a subtle and luminous form that they do not see it or feel it. Yet what men are searching for in women, and what women look for in men is, in reality, only this intangible element. They kiss, and what do they receive? They have not taken something material away from their partner, something they can eat or drink, for instance. And because they do not understand that what they are looking for is not the body – something to hold, to touch, to possess – but a spiritual element, they are always disappointed. This spiritual element which men and women can give to one another is exactly what the love of God is. This love that can be absorbed, that can be breathed, is the only love that leaves no impurities or dissatisfaction. That is why the initiates who have given everything to possess this love are so happy and fulfilled: because they drink from this spring of divine love.

Nourishment is a vast issue because it is not only limited to the food and drink that we consume at every meal. Nourishment can also consist of sounds, smells and colours, as well as feelings and thoughts. Naturally, nourishing yourself in this way is more difficult, but it is possible. On occasion, you can also nourish yourself in this way and, in fact, sometimes you do so without realizing it. You sometimes eat nothing all day without feeling hungry, either because you are totally absorbed, or because you are so filled with love that you feel nourished.

All wisdom, all love, and all spiritual thought is nourishment: they transform themselves into sustenance, even supplying nutriments for your stomach. You can prove this for yourself.

There are occasions when a family man is not able to find enough work in his own country to provide for his family, so he goes to work abroad. He works there for a few years and when he returns, having made a lot of money, he is happy to be able to provide a secure future for his wife and children. He has, however, had to leave them for a certain period of time. The same happens when a spiritual person meditates, prays and unites with God: one could say that he also goes abroad, the difference being that it is not for months or years, but for just a few moments that his spirit distances itself from his physical body. By being too tied down to his body he is not able to do a great deal for himself, so he leaves to earn money or, let us say, to gather light. When he returns he brings this light to his body and to its inhabitants: he illuminates them, enlivens them, purifies them, and regenerates them.

It is said that as Mohammed was walking with one of his disciples one day, a man suddenly stood before them and started to insult the disciple in very crude language. Initially the disciple listened calmly, trying to contain his anger, but very soon, unable to control himself, he was stung into retaliating: they both ended up throwing insult after insult at each other. After a while, when they were both tired, they stopped. However, when the disciple looked around for his master, he could no longer see him. He found him further on, sitting on a street corner. The disciple asked: 'Oh, master, why did you leave me?' and Mohammed answered: 'I do not stand between two angry wild beasts because it is dangerous. When that man was insulting you and you remained silent, invisible beings surrounded you, answering for you and protecting you. But when you too started to shout, trying to defend yourself, these beings left you and I went with them, because your behaviour showed us you did not need us.'

The majority of people have only a mediocre destiny because they seem unable to keep their inner bearings and lose their way: they oscillate incessantly between light and darkness, and that is why their future is always uncertain. Try therefore to channel your energies and direct them towards the luminous world of harmony and love: the divine world. Even if every now and then some shadows appear, it will not be for long: as long as you keep to the right direction within your inner self, there will come a day when you do not wander off the path any more.

Human destiny is governed by precise mathematical laws. Just as your present condition is the result of all you have lived in the past, your future is determined by the direction you give to your life now.

When the sun enters Libra on 23 September it is the autumn equinox[1]. After the ascending phase of the zodiac – from Aries to Virgo, the descending phase starts – from Libra to Pisces.

Libra, or the scales, is the seventh sign of the zodiac. Why are there scales in the sky, and what do they teach us? In the middle of this succession of living creatures, human beings and animals which make up the zodiac, only the scales are a material object or, more accurately, the only instrument. It is as if they held the powers of light and the powers of darkness on each pan: the powers of life and the powers of death. Libra is preceded by Virgo, a young girl carrying heads of corn, and is followed by Scorpio, an animal with a poisonous sting that can kill. This antithesis is emphasised even more by the fact that, within Libra itself, Venus dominates, whilst Saturn is in exaltation. Venus and Saturn, what an association! Venus, a young woman who incarnates grace, harmonious exchanges and pleasure, and Saturn, the austere old man who enjoys solitude and, armed with a scythe, severs the link with life.

Libra is a reflection of cosmic equilibrium, the equilibrium of two opposing but complementary principles, thanks to which the universe was created, and continues to exist.

---

1 In the northern hemisphere. In the southern hemisphere the seasons are reversed, so spring starts on that date. (Editor's note.)

We hear people talk of spiritual love, of noble and disinterested feelings, when they are in fact living in sensuality and the chaos of passion. Others imagine that they have devoted themselves to an ideal, when in reality they are giving free rein to their vanity or their need to dominate others. You will say: 'Well, they are hypocrites, they lack sincerity.' And I say that it may well be that they have true spiritual aspirations, but it is not enough to 'aspire' in order to realize. And if we do not make the effort to enter within our inner self in order to understand the structures and mechanisms of the human psyche, we court the worst contradictions. As in the macrocosm, in the universe, the black head is a reflection in the water of the white Head of God: in this microcosm, which is man, the lower nature is the reflection of the higher nature. The expanse of water is represented in him by the diaphragm, which symbolically separates the higher nature from the lower nature. And as the black head cannot exist without the white Head, conversely, the higher nature and the lower nature within man cannot exist one without the other. It is up to us to understand this clearly, and learn how to put our lower nature to use in order to allow our higher nature to flourish.

The intellect evaluates and draws conclusions on the basis of the appearance of things and on the partial view it has of them. That is why it cannot be relied on to make correct judgments about other people and situations, and that is the origin of many mistakes. Obviously, by accumulating over a long period a large number of elements you can succeed in seeing the complete picture, but how long does that take? There will always be subtle, intangible elements which the intellect cannot grasp. When you first meet someone, you cannot immediately know who he is. It takes a considerable amount of time to get to know him. The only instantaneous way to know a person completely is by developing intuition, which is a manifestation of the spirit. Intuition needs no other element to evaluate: it instantaneously penetrates the heart of people and of things and draws its conclusions immediately, without ever making a mistake. Nothing is hidden from intuition, it alone is able to know people and things as they truly are.

You are having a nightmare, you dream you are being chased, you run and run and then suddenly in front of you there is a ravine and you plunge straight into it. How terrifying! Even when you wake up you continue to live those dramatic events as if they were real. So reflect on these lines: if we can believe a dream to be true, it follows that we can believe reality is a dream. Yes, that is what sages do. Whatever happens to them, they tell themselves: 'I'm suffering, I'm worried, I feel as if I'm being chased, but it's all a dream and when I wake up it will all go away.' You may say that this reasoning will not stop you from suffering. Of course not. But those who have nightmares also suffer: they toss and turn in bed, they cry out, and yet these reactions are triggered by illusory experiences. In fact, that is what they tell themselves when they wake up. So you too, when you suffer, tell yourself it is not true.

Men should not dominate women, and neither should women dominate men. They should, however, each seek to dominate their own sphere. It is normal for women to want to gain freedom and acquire the rights of which men deprived them, but they should try to achieve that by deepening the riches of their own nature, and not by imitating the behaviour and way of life of men.

The balance of nature is based on polarization, that is, on two poles of a different nature – the masculine and the feminine, so exchanges may take place between them. If these poles become uniform, these magnificent exchanges, which are the source of such joy and inspiration, can no longer take place. When men and women have lost the meaning of the life contained in the exchanges between the two poles, they look for remedies in pharmacies or on a psychoanalyst's couch: but there is no cure for those who do not understand. The only remedy can be found by understanding the nature and role of the two principles.

The word 'truth' in Hebrew is 'Emet'. It is made up of three consonants, *Aleph* א, *Mem* מ and *Tav* ת.

Aleph א, the first letter of the alphabet, represents the divine world.

Tav ת, the last letter, represents the physical plane, the basis of all materialization.

Mem מ, the thirteenth letter of the alphabet – which has 22 letters – is therefore near the middle, which represents the spiritual plane, the intermediary world crossed by the ascending and descending forces.

The letter *Mem* מ corresponds to the thirteenth Tarot card. This card depicts a skeleton carrying a scythe: it is death, which cuts down everything perishable. The letter *Mem* מ is therefore a transforming force, destroying everything which is inferior and bad. That is why it is the first letter of the Hebrew word 'Mavèt' meaning 'death', and the first letter of the name of the archangel who takes the soul and leads it to God: Mikhaël.

There is no better cure for fear than love. If you love, fear disappears. Knowledge can also be a cure, but it is not as effective as love, because fear is an instinct and knowledge is not. Instinct can be vanquished or dominated neither by reason nor knowledge nor explanation: it can, however, be vanquished or dominated by another instinct. Reason may sometimes appease fear, but the result is neither long lasting nor certain. Touch someone's heart, however, and he will do anything for you. If a young woman sees a stranger in danger, she may hesitate to save him, but if her loved one is in danger she will be ready to do anything. The disciple should therefore increase the love within himself in order to vanquish fear.

When scientists describe a mineral, a plant, an animal or a human being we cannot fault them; what they say is true. It is only partially true, however. For it to be the whole truth they should situate the object of their study back in the cosmic life to which it belongs. Detached from this life, the stone, the plant, the animal or the person is deprived of the essence. That is why, for as long as scientists continue to work in this way, what they call scientific truth will always be a half-truth, a distorted truth.

Do not misunderstand me: this is not about trying to question the value and benefits of science. The real problem lies elsewhere, in scientists' heads, in their attitudes to life, in their inability to link the objects of their study to life as a whole. Living beings and objects do not exist as separate entities: they exist as part of a whole and these parts are interconnected. A branch, a leaf or a fruit is cut off and studied in isolation. This fruit, however, should be studied whilst still on the tree if we are to understand it as the end result of all the energies circulating in the universe.

Every human being has qualities and virtues that are waiting to manifest. That is why, rather than focusing on the faults of his disciples, a master seeks to bring out all their divine capabilities. That is how I work on you and that is also how you should work, by fostering sacred thoughts for each other. By fostering these sacred thoughts you are no longer waylaid by any less glorious details, so you can concentrate on the divine principle in these beings. You are then doing a good work on your personal evolution, and are also helping others, whereas if you focus on their faults, you harm not only yourself – because you are, as it were, feeding yourself on impurities – but you also hamper others in their personal growth. It is a common mistake to think that you can help others to improve by stressing their faults. The truth is the exact opposite, however: you can only help others by focusing on their divine nature.

Men and women are in the habit of declaring their love without realizing that such behaviour is intertwined with an element of self-interest, of selfishness. They do everything they can to attract, win over, and make a captive of the person whom they are addressing, writing or declaiming as poetically as possible with carefully chosen gestures, words and intonation – and the charmed, touched and delighted addressee ends up being won over.

When love has to be expressed, its purpose is to win over the loved one whilst at the same time preventing another from taking this person away. It is therefore selfishness and lack of faith in the power of love that guides human beings. Since they do not have the true love that works wonders, they rush to express their love by crude means, speaking, writing or gesturing, in order to imprison the person they love. And if they claim that it is the power of their feelings that makes them act in this way, it is really their weakness, passion and sensuality they are emphasizing even more strongly. A true master does not express his love: there is no need, because you can feel his love – it radiates.

He who embarks on initiatic tuition seeking to gain knowledge that will give him power, money and glory, exposes himself to grave danger. What he does not realize is that he is playing the sorcerer's apprentice with the powers of the mind and the soul, and that he will release formidable forces, even within his own body, which he will soon no longer be able to control. We have in the past seen people who have devoted themselves to occult science and who have ended up in trouble, to everyone's surprise. For years these people portrayed an image of wisdom and spirituality: all that concerned them was meditation, thought and study. And then one day, as if an uncontrollable force had taken hold of them, they succumbed to senseless acts of debauchery and violence: the few successes they had achieved had completely turned their heads. What they should have realized, however, is that the more you seek to elevate yourself, the more you must demand of yourself, becoming yet more disinterested and even more humble.

True purity should only serve to help you make ready the dwelling-place of the holy Spirit so that He may come and reside in you, because it is He who will provide the conditions for you to work on the advent of the Kingdom of God on earth. Too many so-called spiritual people still believe that to be pure is to refrain from all contact and shut themselves away in a glass bowl. No. Purity like this, that does nothing, is virtually useless: in fact, it is harmful.

True purity is divine love, because divine love is life: it is water that gushes from the spring, and this gushing water removes everything that is dirty, dull or dark. Even if you are as white as snow, purity without love is not really purity.

So many people think that purity is all about relinquishing love. There are people who are as pure as snow, but they are also as cold as snow. They have no love and their purity is sterile. It is not love from which you should refrain: rather, it is selfish thoughts and feelings you should renounce, because as soon as such feelings arise in you, you are no longer pure. True purity is that of crystal-clear water that springs up, flowing out to irrigate fields and gardens.

All day every day people meet and greet one another, but they greet one another mechanically, distant and indifferent – even within families and between couples. For instance, husband and wife kiss one another goodbye: 'Bye darling ... see you later honey!' But their kiss is empty. They kiss out of habit. Such kisses are not worth anything. You need to be able to give something to the person you kiss in order to invigorate and revive your loved one. Human beings still do not know what it is to kiss, or how and when they should kiss. A husband will seek comfort by hugging and kissing his wife when he is sad or unhappy, and in doing so he passes on his sadness and dejection to his wife. Men and women continually make exchanges, but what do these exchanges consist of? Only God knows, or rather only the devil knows. It is not forbidden to kiss someone, on the contrary, but you must know how and when to kiss in order to impart eternal life.

Why do so many people seek refuge in weakness, sentimentality and over-sensitivity? Instead of thinking, reasoning and trying to find a solution, they respond by taking on a passive attitude: they complain and try their hardest to ensure that everyone else feels sorry for them: 'You poor thing, I understand ... you're so unhappy!' and the result is that the intensity of their sobbing redoubles. It is the same with children: a child falls and hurts himself and starts to cry. If you say: 'Oh, darling, how awful, you're hurt', he will cry even more. If, however, you say: 'Look, you're all right, you can carry on playing', he will dry his tears and soon forget all about it.

So many adults are like children: they cry about anything, and everyone around them – in all ignorance and thinking they are being kind – starts to comfort them. What sense is there in that? You must use your intelligence if you want to help others, otherwise all you do is encourage them to sink deeper into their weaknesses.

Binah is the first Sephirah on the left pillar of the Sephirotic Tree, the Pillar of Severity, the feminine principle in creation, where God manifests Himself under the name of Jehovah. He is the awesome God who revealed Himself to Moses. His anger, his menaces and the curses that would punish human beings until the fourth generation, resound throughout the whole of the Old Testament.

You wonder: 'How can this awesome God be a feminine power?' Because this feminine power represents nature in reality. This concept is easier to understand if you think about what nature really is: an implacable mother. Nature has its laws and if you go against these laws, you are punished in some way or other. And, by inference, this punishment will affect your children and your grandchildren. Let us take the well-known example of alcoholism. He who abuses alcohol not only harms his physical and mental health, but also passes on a tainted heredity. The same goes for other types of abuse and transgression. Really, it is so simple.

Good and evil are so closely intertwined that we have to think very carefully before seeking to separate them. Any premature separation causes wrenching and tearing. Successful separation is a most difficult art and initiates take their instruction from nature itself. We are not able to separate the nut from its husk, but nature knows how to do so: she allows the fruit to ripen and the husk comes away by itself and falls off. This separation is a sign of maturity.

The child is attached to its mother's bosom. Taking it away prematurely would result in death for both. If, however, you allow the fruit time to fall off by itself, the tie between the mother and the child can be cut.

Initiates, who have observed nature, say: 'Your soul is a prisoner; to free it you must separate away the thick layer that surrounds it, but you must first wait until it has matured.' Autumn is the best time to meditate on true liberation.

Many people take extraordinary pleasure in talking about the most negative and least pleasant details of their lives and are then surprised when their friends avoid or abandon them. What a ludicrous way to live! It is best if you hide this kind of information. Be aware that others cannot really help you resolve your problems: they have their own, which they find difficult enough to solve. So why burden them with yours? Not only are you wasting your time by needlessly telling them your business, but you actually lower their esteem for you and eventually they no longer value you: they come to realize that you have no wisdom or self-control and they drop you. If you do not want to lose your friends, hide your troubles from them, tell them nothing, do not complain. Learn instead to form a bond with all the celestial powers, with all the luminous entities that are there ready to help you. It is they who will really help you.

What we call life is nothing more than the result of exchanges in which we engage with nature. Life is a series of exchanges. The most obvious manifestations of this are nourishment and breathing. Any kind of interference in these exchanges results in weakness, illness and death. However, the exchanges we must make in order to live are not limited to feeding ourselves and breathing. Or rather, we can say that they consist of feeding ourselves and breathing, but not merely on the physical plane. Nutrition and breathing symbolize the exchanges we also have to make with the different spheres of the universe in order to feed our subtle bodies: the etheric, astral, mental, causal, buddhic and atmic bodies[1].

When you understand how you can find in the universe the nourishment that suits your different bodies, you will experience your life as a great symphony. First, however, you must re-establish communications in order to allow the energy currents to circulate between the universe and yourself. And you can only re-establish communications by working with thought.

---

1 See note and diagram pages 366-367

In order to understand love truly, we must first admit that, contrary to what most people think, love is not a feeling – because a feeling is inevitably subject to variations depending on the person to whom the feeling is directed – but a state of consciousness that is independent of people and circumstances. To love is therefore not to have a feeling for someone, but to do everything with love: talking, walking, eating, breathing, studying, with love. It is to have reconciled all our organs, all our cells and all our faculties so that they vibrate in unison in light and peace. All the manifestations of our being are then impregnated with divine waves and fluids. Love is a permanent state of consciousness: day and night, we live in this state of joy and expansion in which everything we do is a melody.

The masculine principle and the feminine principle are physically present in the bodies of all human beings. In fact both principles are present in their mouths. The tongue is the masculine principle and the lips are the feminine principle, and together they have a child: speech. That is why the only true power of human beings lies in speech. Indeed, human beings can achieve as much by speech alone as by any other material means. We can build and destroy; we can gather and we can separate; we can restore peace and we can start a war; we can heal and we can make unwell. When the primitive androgyne divided into two, it could be said that, symbolically, woman kept the lips – the feminine principle, and man kept the tongue – the masculine principle. This is why, in order now to retrieve their original power, they seek to unite. Yes, from there stems this age-old impulse that makes men and women seek each other out.

Even if this takes the form of pleasure or diversion, its fundamental purpose is to seek out the unity of the Word, the unity of the creative principle, which is both male and female.

Human beings have got into the habit of busying their intellect to such an extent and often in such a disorganised way that they are no longer in control of their thoughts. And it is this utterly disorganised, cacophonous thinking that prevents them from elevating themselves beyond the astral and mental[1] planes, and sense heaven.

If we want to taste the realities of the spiritual world we must learn to stop our thought process. The wise men of India claimed that the intellect is the assassin of reality. And it is true: our intellect allows us to obtain a great deal of information superficially, but we will never get to know the reality, the quintessence. It is the heart which has been granted the capacity to penetrate reality. However, to initiates the heart is not the physical heart, nor even feeling. When they speak of 'the intelligence of the heart', what they actually mean is the soul, and it is the soul alone that has the capacity to feel the deep reality of things.

---

1 See note and diagram pages 366-367

So many people complain about the sinful nature of mankind, about how human beings carry the seed of evil within them. There is nothing to complain about, however. All we have to do is work. Whether it be vanity, pride, anger, jealousy, sensuality, all faults must be put to work. That is the only way to look at things, the only good solution. Work is what counts. Do not concern yourself with anything else – your qualities or your faults. They are of secondary importance.

When you have found the best work for you, and when you have decided to commit yourself to that work truthfully, all those apparent faults and failings will become your most faithful servants. Let us take a very simple example: you want to pick up a weight. All the energies that produce the power of your physical body are there to give you a helping hand: muscles, heart, lungs, and even your brain assist in the act. If, however, you do not wish to do anything at all, all your organs are put out of action. It is work that stimulates all your potential. Through work a criminal can, eventually, outdo the most virtuous people in generosity, patience and goodness. Whereas those people who are generally thought to be the most outstanding, achieve very little, because the idea of work does not enter their minds.

You are always dwelling on past mistakes and sufferings but, instead, try to look to the future. Think that you are the son or daughter of God and that your destiny is to come ever closer to your celestial Father, to manifest his qualities. Imagine this extraordinary state of blossoming, joy and fulfilment, and already you will be able to taste your destiny, you will live it, and you will have made it real.

When you are faced with an experience you dread – sitting an exam, undergoing surgery, appearing before a court – you worry for several days beforehand wondering how it will work out. And when you think you are about to meet your loved one, you can already feel the joy. So, if thought can make you anticipate the very near future with pleasure, or otherwise, then why not the far distant future, also? The power of imagination is a reality, and all disciples must learn to use it to speed up their evolution.

It is not enough to send a child to school to educate him, however good that school may be. If at home the parents expose their child to their arguments, their lies and their dishonesty, how can they imagine they are capable of educating him? It has been shown that the parents' arguments can cause a baby to show symptoms of anxiety and become ill, even if the infant was not present at the time. The reason is that these arguments create such an atmosphere of disharmony that the child absorbs it, because the tie with the parents is still very strong. The baby is not aware of this, but his etheric[1] body receives the shocks.

Some parents' behaviour is so unbelievable that you cannot help but wonder whether they really love their children. These parents, of course, will claim that they do love their children; but they do not. If they loved them, they would change their attitude. They would at least try to overcome some of those weaknesses that affect their children so adversely. If they do not make this effort, it is proof that they do not really love their children.

---

1 See note and diagram pages 366-367

Before launching yourself into all kinds of psychical experiences that may put you in danger, first work at becoming a real master of yourself, taking care to watch carefully over your desires and your aspirations. Only then will you be sure you will be able to defend yourself, even if you are exposed to danger, because the perils that you encounter in the psychic world are as numerous and deadly – if not more so – than those of the physical world. If you did not first work to prepare yourselves you will be vulnerable, and then you will find yourselves in such a state that all you can do is to shout and go around complaining to everyone about your experiences. So many so-called spiritual people have ended up victims of the entities and forces they have foolishly called forth. They believe they are being followed by monsters: they live in hell. Of course they do not understand how this has happened to them. It is quite simple, however: by seeking to penetrate the astral[1] world for all the wrong reasons – curiosity and cupidity – they have attracted entities which have made them live, really, in hell. Because that is what hell is: the lower astral world.

[1] See note and diagram pages 366-367

Life is a rich source of learning for human beings. Sages think about everything, learn about everything, and use everything to do good. On the other hand, others are unable to benefit from anything, even if good things come their way. Not only are they unable to see and use these good things, but they even manage to organize things in such a way that all this good is turned against them.

If you are aware, if you are vigilant, even your failures and misfortune can contribute to your personal growth, because you will know how to make use of them. You will tell yourself: 'Good! Here is another great opportunity to become stronger, wiser and more spiritual,' and the more opportunities you get, the stronger you will become. If you do not have these opportunities you will never grow. These misfortunes play the same role as exams or competitions – forcing people to practise and develop.

When you have experienced a moment of great joy, expect to find things starting to go wrong, or to experience unpleasantness from the people around you. Yes, be on your guard, because if you are not, if you are insouciant or careless, you will be taken by surprise. When you are fortunate enough to experience some moments of happiness, do not let yourself go: be vigilant, because the negative side is already getting ready to pounce and if you let yourself be taken unawares, all the advantages you have gained may be lost. This is the law. Since everything is interlinked, when a movement occurs in one area, it automatically starts up an inverse movement elsewhere.

Anyone who enjoys throwing pieces of broken glass on the road, saying: 'It doesn't matter! I won't be around, so it will only harm others,' is mistaken, because the road we follow is not a straight line. You may not be aware of this, but the path along which we human beings travel is a circular one. He who has scattered broken glass will, therefore, one day have to walk along the same stretch of road where previously he spread danger, and will have to suffer the consequences of his actions. If you dig holes or set traps along the road, the laws will take you past that very spot again and make you fall into these same holes and into these same traps. And then you will have time to reflect on your misadventure, to grumble about people's wickedness and stupidity, and try to discover who the culprits are. You will, of course, have forgotten that the culprit was you, yourself. He who lives with a devil-may-care attitude creates all the problems which will, one day, plague his life.

Every man and woman carries in their heart, in their soul, an ideal image of the person whom they want to love, indeed, have a need to love. They imagine this person in a more or less confused way, and when, during the course of their lives, they meet a person with whom they start to have a relationship, subconsciously they are seeking to compare that person with the picture they carry deep within themselves. This ideal that lives in the head of every man and every woman is that of their kindred spirit – their soul mate. If you succeed in becoming sufficiently aware, you will find that the attraction or repulsion you feel for different people throughout your life has its origin in the picture you carry hidden deep within your soul.

Whatever the trials and tribulations in your life, never lose control of yourself, but instead try, within yourself, to right the wrongs. Even if you cannot make everything better, through thought you are creating a tiny seed which is already beginning to bear fruit. And even if you find yourself totally, one hundred per cent, out in the cold and dark, at least you will only be ninety-nine per cent out there, because you have prayed, you have concentrated on a luminous image: and that is a cry for someone to come and help you.

You do not observe life around you, and learn from it. Take a child for instance: who taught him, who informed him that the power of speech is a true strength? When a child is in danger, he screams: 'Mummy!' How has that child learned to use a magical word? If he had not shouted, his mother would not have known he was in danger. However, she does hear him and rushes to help him. So why do we not, at least, call out to heaven for help when we have problems or are in danger?

What are people's main preoccupations today? Food, clothes, housing, earning money, getting married and having a few children. Everything revolves around self-satisfaction and personal well-being. Of course, every now and then they do something for society, but on the whole they do things for their own benefit. However, whether they like it or not, they live in a collectivity, and if a revolution, a riot or a war breaks out within this collectivity, their personal possessions cannot be secure. So, even if they make sure that everything in their lives is organized, in reality everything is never organized, because problems can always arise from the collectivity and destroy everything. Indeed, throughout history this is repeatedly evident. There were people who were so rich and powerful that nothing seemed to be able to touch them, that is, until troubles arose within society and they ended up losing everything, even their lives. Everyone must therefore seek to improve collective life: that is the only condition in which every individual can feel secure, because only collective life, which encompasses everything, is able to provide security and plenty for everyone.

The disciple must take measures in order to ensure that his lower nature does not get the better of his divine nature. When he succeeds in a particular area, he must tell himself: 'It is not I who deserve the credit, but You, Lord,' otherwise he risks falling into the trap of arrogance. When you receive praise or you are being congratulated, be on your guard, do not allow yourself to become swollen-headed, but keep saying to yourself: 'It is not I who deserve the glory, but You, Lord.' Other people often unintentionally set you traps, and you could take their compliments so seriously that you become arrogant and pretentious, which poses a threat to your personal evolution. You must work for the glory of God, and if you are praised, transfer this praise on to Him: that is how your impersonal, disinterested side can develop. Heaven appraises you according to your attitude in order to know in whose name you work. Nothing is more important for a disciple's true glory than glorifying the Lord.

If the word 'to know' is understood to mean the result of the perceptions gained from our five senses, human beings cannot know God, because what is limited cannot know that which is unlimited. Human beings will know God when they enter immensity, when they unite with Him and become part of Him. So long as a drop of water is separated from the ocean, it cannot know it, but when it returns to the ocean, it can no longer separate itself from it; it has become the ocean and so knows it. Therefore, so long as human beings remain separate from God, they cannot understand the immensity and infinity of God. They must merge with Him, unite with Him, lose themselves in Him, and only then will they know Him, because they become Him, they are Him. So long, however, as they remain outside God, they cannot know Him and they will continue to ask questions about His existence.

The Elohim, the Angels of the Sephirah Netzach[1], created the world and this cosmic event is reproduced on the human level every time a man and a woman conceive a child. In order to create a child, the man and the woman are under the influence of Netzach, love, and the Elohim build the body of this child. Even if the man and the woman are not aware of this, the Elohim are at work. The Sephiroth are sublime regions, but every day they are at work in all spheres of life. Yes, just look at how a child is created: the Elohim are there, the father and the mother have called upon them, and a few months later a small human being appears and everyone is filled with wonder. Without knowing it human beings work together with cosmic forces, with magical forces. What magical forces are more powerful than those of procreation? Magic can let loose hurricanes, but that is nothing compared with the creation of a living being.

1 See note and diagram pages 366-367

Thought and love allow you to work with all of nature to make it open up its secrets to you. Try it: when you are standing by a lake, a forest or a mountain, pause for a moment and give a sign of acknowledgement with your hand. Inside you will start to feel an equilibrium, a harmony, and much uncertainty and incomprehension will leave you, simply because you have decided to salute living nature and the creatures that inhabit her. Just touch a stone with love and that stone changes, it is no longer the same, it accepts you, it vibrates in unison with you, it loves you too.

Yes, everything on earth is alive, and it is up to you to know how to work to make this life come to you. The day you succeed in relating consciously with creation, you will feel true life penetrating you.

Learn to look upon men and women with a feeling of sacredness, and behind their appearance and behind the shape of their body or their face you will discover their soul and their spirit which are the son and daughter of God. If you can let your attention rest on their soul and their spirit, all God's creatures that you have neglected, abandoned and despised in the past will seem extremely precious. Heaven, which sent them on earth in all kinds of disguises, looks upon them as treasures, as receptacles of Divinity. So, whenever you meet anyone, instead of focusing on their physical appearance, their wealth, their position or their education, look at their soul and their spirit, otherwise you will never come to know their quintessence. Tell yourself that, in the eyes of God who created them, even those who walk around on earth as beggars or tramps are princes and princesses.

People harbour so many impurities that it is they themselves who block their entrance to paradise. Those who work to regain their original purity, however, will one day hear God Himself calling to them: 'Come on in and look around!' And what will these people see? They will see bodies of light. In paradise everyone is naked, clothed only in light. Light is the only garment worn by angels because the very substance of their bodies is light.

In the mysteries of antiquity the goddess Isis wore a veil which only the high priests and the hierophants were allowed to remove. This means that the man who wishes to behold the Divinity must be naked, in other words pure, otherwise the Divinity will always remain veiled from his eyes and Her secrets forever hidden from him. To the extent that man becomes more pure, so Isis reveals herself to him, and then he sees, understands, and experiences extraordinary joy. That is true paradise.

Why do people go and see a master, an initiate? To tell him of their misfortunes and their problems in the expectation that he will sort out everything and work miracles on their behalf. People should understand that an initiate can do nothing for those who come to him with their complaints, without making any efforts to resolve their own problems. He will not perform miracles for them. Life itself will teach them lessons and, unfortunately, those lessons will be terrible.

Human beings are pig-headed: they insist on sticking to their convictions and then, when they are faced with failure, they complain loudly without understanding that this failure stems from their refusal to bring themselves into harmony with the laws of nature. They all yell: 'I want this! I want that!' and set to energetically to get what they want. The laws of nature, however, are not in agreement with this attitude and refuse to gratify such indiscriminate wishes. The problem is that human beings refuse to understand. They stubbornly insist on satisfying these desires until such time as they are prostrate with exhaustion. Why do they refuse to understand?

A noise wakes you up in the night: the phone rings, something falls, someone knocks at the door. Do you immediately jump out of bed in the dark? No, because you know it is risky. The first thing you do before you take action is to turn on the light so you can see. Well, you must realize that you must also first turn on the light before anything you may do, whatever it may be and whatever the circumstance, so you can see what you are doing. And to turn on the light means you must concentrate, you must collect your thoughts and seek help from heaven so as to know the best course of action. Without this light you are lost: you explore every avenue, you have a go at every possible venture, but all is in vain. Never forget the essential: to turn on the light, because the light will help you avoid incurring a great deal of damage and wasting much time.

It is said in Genesis: 'God created humankind in his image, in the image of God he created them; male and female he created them.' Which means, according to the Zohar, that God created Adam, primordial man, as male and female, in other words having both principles. You will say: 'And what about Eve? It is written that then God created Eve.' Yes, God took the feminine principle from the masculine principle. He objectified her before Him. The meaning of this image of God taking one of Adam's ribs and making it into Eve has greatly preoccupied theologians.

Adam and Eve are not a man and a woman. They are symbols. Adam is the masculine principle, who begat Eve, the feminine principle. And what does that mean? That the first principle came out of his state of extreme subtleness in order to condense, and in so doing he created another principle, Eve. It is said in Genesis that Adam was created before Eve because Moses, who was an initiate, knew that the masculine principle always manifests first. He is first because he is the creative principle: he is the basis of creation and therefore also the basis of all matter. Matter is a condensation of the power of the spirit which Moses describes by means of an image: Eve drawn from one of Adam's ribs. Matter is a condensation of the forces of the spirit and that is why, symbolically, the feminine principle always comes after the masculine principle.

All the rites established by the Church should not obscure true religion. People often put on the 'tinted spectacles' of a religion, a philosophy or a coterie, and they end up losing sight of everything else. What is the use of religion if it hides the splendour of what God has created and obscures the possibility of returning to the Godhead?

The clergy has warped people to such an extent that it is now no longer possible to make them understand the marvels of creation. What they have created themselves, yes, this they understand; but they have no interest whatsoever in what God has created, because that is not worthy of their attention. Of course they would not say so outright, but in practice it is just as if they were considering themselves superior to God. Instead of saying: 'Respect life, children, because everything is sacred; so honour the talismans which God has piaced everywhere.' All that matters to the clergy is their tools: the dogma, the rituals, the reliquaries, the rosaries, and the medals; the rest of creation is of no importance.

Many men and women feel they have been thrown into a strange or even hostile world. Why? Because they have lost touch with nature. They have lost that feeling of friendship, of well-being with all that surrounds them: the plants, the rocks, the animals, the sun, the stars, etc. Even when they are in the shelter of their own homes they are worried and troubled. Even in their sleep they feel threatened.

This feeling is subjective, however, because in truth nothing really threatens them, but inside something has started to disintegrate and they no longer feel protected. They therefore need to put their inner selves back in touch with universal life so as to understand its language and to work in harmony with it.

Heaven only gives credit to those who deserve it. When people are seen to be making sincere and disinterested efforts, trying to serve with all their heart and soul, heaven cannot but give credit, so it pours out all its blessings on them. On the other hand, people who use their gifts from heaven for their own benefit, or to do wrong, receive no credit: heaven withholds all blessings from them. That is why all spiritual traditions urge people to make good use of the gifts, qualities and riches they have been given, otherwise sooner or later heaven will take back all those same gifts, qualities and riches: they may have distinguished themselves brilliantly in this life, but they will find themselves poor and naked in the next.

Human beings seek love, wealth and glory, but what they are really searching for in all this is God, because in reality nothing or nobody can bring them joy except God. Yes, in one way or another people are always looking for the Divinity; they always yearn to return to the Source to find again their provenance, their original life immersed in paradise. Unfortunately the poor souls are not enlightened so they walk many a muddy road and squelch around in the mud, bogging themselves down inextricably; and who knows when they will reach their goal? Since God has put a small particle of his quintessence in every thing and in every being, we can find Him everywhere. However, since most people disperse themselves here there and everywhere, they will need billions of years in their search for God. The straight road to God must pass along the paths of purity and light.

When you do everything possible to lose your self-control by allowing yourself to be taken over by lower entities whose only interest lies in destroying human beings, no one else is to blame but you. What you should say is: 'All right, so I did not work properly! I did not study well!' and you should rectify the situation by getting yourself under control again. Of course it will take some time. If you have spent years in a turmoil of confused thoughts and feelings, you cannot expect everything to settle calmly into place within a few days. You will have to work for a long time to get results. Human beings do not know the laws: they live foolishly for years, and when they eventually decide to change their ways they imagine it can be done in just a few minutes. Unfortunately that is impossible, whatever they may think. Just as it has taken considerable time to destroy themselves, so it takes an equally great deal of time for them to recover.

Words are a two-edged weapon, able to enlighten, help and liberate, as well as to destroy and massacre. Often when people have destroyed someone with reproach and recriminations they claim to have done so, 'For that person's own good. He needed to hear it. I was only being honest.' In truth, however, such people need to express their irritation, or dissatisfaction and they use 'a person's own good' and 'honesty' as a pretext. Why can they only be honest under the influence of anger? They may give all the reasons they like, but people cannot have a good influence on others by means of words until their motivation is truly disinterested and spiritual.

It is quite extraordinary how today you can find initiates everywhere you go, even in clubs and other such haunts. And how do you recognize them? Well, it is quite simple, because they themselves proclaim: 'I am an initiate!' Some even add that they have reached the seventh, eighth or ninth level of initiation; much to the delight of the naïve and undiscerning who imagine they have found a real live initiate able to award them with initiatic diplomas within a just few days.

In the past the identity of an initiate was hidden from all except those who were sincerely searching, and possessed true discernment. The fact that they were were initiates was never vaunted: they remained private, unknown, hidden, like the Hermit on the ninth Tarot card. The old man holding a lamp, shielding it in the folds of his large coat to screen it from the crowd's eyes – that is the image of a true initiate.

You think it normal to allow your emotions, excitement, and passion to get the better of you, but do you ever give a thought to the state of your brain when you have to reflect on solutions to important problems, or understand fundamental issues? You do not. What a detrimental way to behave! If you want your brain to be always strong and ready for use, you must be attentive, careful, economical and measured in everything you do, otherwise you will understand nothing and, moreover, you will be too tired to comprehend even if the greatest of life's secrets were revealed to you; and this would be a shame, a very great shame. That is why you should try not to waste time and energy on preoccupations which will only weaken you. Then, when truths with the power to set you free appear, you will be wide awake and clear-headed and able to grasp them instantaneously.

When people are asked if they would like to live in heaven, the majority will say: 'Well yes, of course!' What they do not know is that you must prepare yourself if you want to live in heaven. You cannot live in the higher regions if you do not possess the means, otherwise you will be there for only a moment before running back to earth saying: 'But they don't have cigarettes there – not even pubs, or clubs! And I want to smoke. I want to drink. I want to kiss pretty women. I want to go back down.' If you wish to live in sublime regions, you should not have such crude needs. That is why not everybody is ready to live in heaven. Even if people are put there forcibly, they will soon leave complaining: 'It's quite unbearable, you die here!' That is no reason, however, not to try to adapt to divine life. For millions of years humanity has evolved on earth and if you make the effort to practise meditation every day, putting to work cells in certain areas of your brain, you will go very far – so far, in fact, that eventually you will make your home in the divine world.

You are children of the twentieth century and the twentieth century is said to be the century of progress. Yes, technological progress, that is indeed true: when it comes to technological progress human beings have indeed accomplished wonders. But what is technological progress? A victory over physical matter. So, what do human beings do then? Satisfied and proud of themselves for having managed to produce all kinds of equipment and products which make their lives easier, they do not realize that they then use these same technological advances to feed their lower nature, satisfying their selfish egos, laziness, sensuality and aggressive behaviour. Well, that is not progress. It is regression. Try to analyze yourself: watch how you use everything technological progress has made available and you will discover that rarely, indeed very rarely, is it used for your spiritual evolution and for the good of others. Why? Because in order to be able to profit truly from all the riches provided for us in physical matter, we must first work on the mental, emotional and spiritual planes. Technological progress will become true progress only when people make use of this technology at the same time as trying to live in a spiritual way.

Fire is the most powerful element, therefore provides the most effective means of purification and transformation. Nothing withstands fire. That is why initiatic tradition teaches that if people want to transform themselves, they must pass through fire.

There are two types of fire: the fire of suffering and the fire of divine love. Through the fire of suffering must pass all those who so stubbornly and obstinately insist in taking the wrong road that only trials can make them reflect and change direction. Do you wish to escape this fire of suffering? Then you must work with the fire of love, which will make you glow with radiant light. Here on earth we cannot escape trials, so even if we still have to endure suffering, we shall overcome these trials thanks to the flames of divine love burning ever more intensely within us. The fire of ordinary suffering enslaves people: the fire of divine love liberates them.

Every day life presents us with complex situations and we need to learn to be flexible in order to cope with them. There are people who react in the same way to every circumstance, using the same means, the same methods, whatever the situation. However, since every problem has its own specific solution, these people never stop running full tilt into obstacles. You need to be flexible, and flexibility is all about being more of a psychologist, more of an educationalist, more of a diplomat – but not a diplomat in the pejorative sense of hypocritical and sly. True diplomacy implies wisdom. The sage is a diplomat who knows the most beneficial method to choose to do maximum good in every given situation, or vis-a-vis any individual. A sage, a true sage, thinks and finds ways to manoeuvre like a sailor who knows the currents and reefs, and knows how to steer his craft to avoid shipwreck. Flexibility therefore implies wisdom. To be flexible in life means to have wisdom and psychological insight.

Learn to live in harmony with the great cosmic body – the universe, because this harmony embraces all that is good: health, joy, light and inspiration. If you work toward achieving this harmony, you will begin to feel the whole of your being vibrating in unison with the universe and you will understand the meaning of life, creation, love, and so on. But not before. Without this harmony it is impossible to understand. Intellectually, externally, you can always imagine that you have grasped some small ideas, but true understanding is not a product of the brain: it comes through the whole body, even through your feet, your arms, stomach, liver, etc. The whole body must understand in every one of its cells. True understanding is a sensation. You feel and then you understand, and you know – because you have tasted the flavour of harmony. No intellectual understanding can compare with sensation.

Whatever the field in which you study or work, you must put life at the centre and see this life in its highest, greatest dimension. Then, once you are focused on the quintessence you can allow yourself to set out and explore every area you wish. If you have already concentrated on this essential work, depending on the extent of your efforts, all that you subsequently do benefits from that light and takes on a different dimension. Not only does your intellect provide you with clearer knowledge, but also a whole deep, inner process of regeneration is unleashed because you are once again in touch with the whole. You are in communion with the subtle currents of the universe; you are in the midst of cosmic life; you take part in this life in harmony with all other visible and invisible creatures, and your field of consciousness widens.

Is it not true to say that you love people showing you consideration? In fact, you feel it is only normal. So why are you not considerate to every being, to every thing? Try, even, to show how much you appreciate every flower when you plant it or water it. You may say that a flower feels nothing. Well, that is exactly where you are mistaken. Furthermore, it is for your own benefit that you should appreciate this flower because you are the one who will acquire some virtue and merit. You make a considerate gesture of respect or love towards someone, and that gesture reflects on you. You need to apply yourself for years to all these small things and then, one day, you will reap the benefits. Do not go looking elsewhere, far away, for what is already nearby. You will never find the solution to your problems somewhere outside your everyday activities. If you neglect these daily occupations, the invisible world will make you return to them and rub your nose in them until you have learned to understand this truth.

Every living creature has a passive feminine side, which symbolizes darkness, and an active masculine side, which symbolizes light. The light must penetrate the darkness in order to illuminate it and extract its many riches.

In us, for instance, the intellect represents the light and the heart represents the dark. The intellect penetrates the heart (ours and that of others) in order to illuminate it and work with it. To use an image, one could say that the intellect must penetrate and withdraw from the heart in the way a piston moves up and down. If you do not use your intellect in this way, you are incapable of understanding anything and are, above all, incapable of knowing yourself. By penetrating the deep chasm of the heart with its light, wisdom finds all the treasures hidden there – seams of precious stones, metals and priceless liquids. Into the dark well of the heart the intellect descends and comes back up, descends and rises again, extracting supplies of the heart's precious water.

The Creator has given us qualities and gifts and, one day, we will be called to account for the way in which we have used them. You know the parable in the Gospel of the three servants whose master, before his departure, entrusted them with money. To the first he gave three talents, to the second he gave one, and to the third he gave five. When he returned he asked them how they had used this money. The servants who had been given several talents had used their money profitably, but the servant who had received just one had buried it in the ground. This servant the master punished, and the other two he rewarded.

Heaven will demand that we account for the qualities, gifts and virtues we have been given. Are they withered away because we neglected them? Did they bear fruit because we used them well? According to how we have acted we shall be either rewarded or punished.

A true master is someone who has worked for thousands of years to overcome all his passionate human desires and to attract the blessings of heaven. That is why he emanates elements which benefit all those around him. And this is the advantage of meeting a master: by living near him, by listening to him, his disciples receive a small fragment of the life he emanates which enables them to evolve much more rapidly. Otherwise of what use would a master be? He is not concerned with giving you wealth, jobs or women. His concern is to give you particles of a higher nature which vibrate in harmony with heaven. And if you can receive these particles, if you can keep hold of them and even amplify them, in time you will feel your thoughts, your feelings and even your health improve. In the proximity of a true master you can only find blessings.

Human beings, like animals, must eat to live, but unlike animals, human beings can, through their greater awareness, find in their nourishment a way to develop mentally, spiritually and emotionally. And I would go even further: as long as human beings are not capable of giving the act of eating a greater and deeper dimension, it is pointless for them to claim to be civilized or cultured. That is my criterion. When human beings learn to eat with enlightened consciousness, filled with wonder at the food they eat, thinking with gratitude of how the entire universe has worked to produce the fruit, vegetables and grain which give them life – then, and only then, can we consider ourselves to be civilized and cultured.

A spirit, a soul, is linked to a body for one lifetime. At the time of death they separate from the body and, later, in a subsequent reincarnation another union is made. The human ego is neither man nor woman: it is by incarnating on earth that it becomes one or the other, depending on whether it is polarized positively or negatively. If it is polarized positively it generally incarnates in a feminine form in order to have both principles and, inversely, if it is polarized negatively, it takes on the body of a man. And you ask: 'What determines this polarization of the human ego?' Well, it all depends on the degree of evolution of each individual ego and the work it has to do to reach perfection.

Our incarnation on earth is already in some way a form of marriage. We could therefore say that the first marriage a human being enters into is that of his ego with his physical body, and *that* marriage demands absolute fidelity.

You may pray fervently that someone be saved, but if sometimes you receive no answer, it is because it would upset all heaven's plans if your request were granted. Let us suppose that you have a friend who is unwell and you pray that he or she may soon recover. You pray ardently for him or her and your prayer is strong because it is sincere. However, the edict of the beings up above is as follows: 'We need to create new, different connections in this person to help him understand certain facts which will help him behave more appropriately in the future. To achieve this, we must immobilize him for some time. That is why we have confined him to bed and bound him hand and foot so he cannot move. We therefore refuse to grant this prayer because it asks for him to be released from illness before we have completed our work.' When someone is unwell it is difficult to know whether he or she is suffering from a real illness or whether the invisible world is working to speed up his or her evolution.

If it is customary to pray to the Lord by lighting a candle or burning incense, it is because a burning candle and incense are symbols of sacrifice, of transformation from a raw material to a more subtle one: light and fragrance. Nothing people do in their lives is mere chance. Even things that appear insignificant have a deep meaning. Each time you light a fire or a candle you must be struck by the depth of this phenomenon of sacrifice, and you must reflect that the upper planes of the soul and the spirit will become accessible to you only on condition that something within yourself is burned in exchange. There are so many disparate things accumulated within us which we can burn. All the impurities, all the selfish tendencies, all the inclinations towards passionate desire, these are what we must burn to generate light; and this light will never leave us.

Nature spreads all its riches before us and we are entitled to help ourselves provided we give something in return. You are surprised that all this is not free? It is free, but you too must give freely in exchange. How? Well, when you decide to use all the faculties which God has given you to walk consciously along the road of light and sacrifice, you are thus engaged in the service of the Lord; so God remunerates you by giving you intelligence, goodness, beauty, etc. And it is with this 'money' that you can 'pay' for all that you take from nature. If you are not engaged in the service of heaven you get nothing, and are therefore impoverished, with no 'money' to pay for what you take. You eat, you drink, you breathe, you walk around, you make transactions, but sooner or later the creditors – the forces of nature – come to take everything away, because negligence, laziness, disrespect and ingratitude are not acceptable payment. So then the creditors take their 'money' from the flesh and the bones of their debtor: they take his or her life.

In the dialogue 'The Banquet' Plato recounts the myth of the primitive androgyne. In days long gone by, human creatures are said to have lived on earth who were both male and female: they were spherical in shape and had two faces, four arms, four legs, two genital organs, etc. These creatures had exceptional vigour and, conscious of their power, they undertook to attack the gods. Greatly concerned, the latter sought a way to weaken them and it was Zeus who found the answer: they would be cut in two. This was done and that is why, ever since then, these two halves of one divided being roam the world continuously looking for each other in order to unite, and so refind their initial integrity.

In Plato's myth one detail is particularly significant: in order to weaken these creatures threatening the power of the gods, Zeus decided to split them in half. The conclusion is clear: the power of human beings depends on the possession of both principles. Human beings are akin to gods when they possess both principles – masculine and feminine.

Most human beings are so limited in their love that when a man and woman meet they forget the entire world: nothing else exists as far as they are concerned. They are not yet used to understanding love in a wider sense, so they impoverish and mutilate love. It is no longer a divine love springing forth, showering down upon all creatures. True love is love which embraces all creatures without limitation, without putting down its roots with one person alone. That is why men and women should be taught to embrace wider concepts, to show less possessiveness and jealousy. The husband should find joy in seeing his wife love the world as a whole, and the wife should also be happy that her husband has such a big heart. When two truly evolved people get married they have allowed each other this mutual freedom beforehand. Each one finds joy in being able to love all creatures with the greatest purity. The wife understands her husband and the husband understands his wife, and they are mutually uplifted, walking together towards heaven, because they are living the true, unlimited life.

If ancient religions and civilizations have not been able to withstand the ravages of time and have disappeared, it proves that their values were incapable of creating new life: their forms became crystallized and fossilized, and the spirit swept away their old, degenerating structures. Do not, therefore, linger amongst ruins. Do not look for rubble upon which to found your religion. Many spiritual people seek to return to ancient initiations. That is a mistake. You should not awaken the mysteries of the past because even from a spiritual point of view it is dangerous to try to reanimate what is already dead. Instead of dwelling on the past, reach out to the future, because what your future will be is, in fact, the present of the higher beings watching over you. And so, by receiving what these beings give you, you speed up your evolution.

Do spiritual people carry weight in society? No. Why is that? Because they are not united. They either do not know each other or they are hostile towards each other. They do not believe they will cooperate together in some way. On the other hand, look at what materialists undertake and what they achieve! As for scientists ... from an initiatic point of view it may be true that they are mistaken, that they do not have a high ideal nor a true overview of things, and are unable to direct their researches towards the best objective: but they do work together, they support each other, they help each other, they inform each other of their discoveries, and that is why they have such power in the world. So when will spiritual people decide to unite to work together for the good of humanity?

Your future will turn out to be what you are building in the present. It is therefore the ‘now’ that counts. The future is an extension of the present, and the present is nothing more than a consequence, a result of the past. Everything is linked: the past, the present and the future are not separate. The future will be built on the foundations you are laying now. If these foundations are not good, there is obviously no point in expecting an exceptional future, but if they are good, then there is of course no need to worry. The roots determine the nature of the trunk, the branches and the fruit. The past is past, but it has brought about the present, and the present forms the roots of the future. You are, therefore, building your future by seeking to improve the present.

Even if they are not aware of it, people who deny the existence of entities higher than themselves are limiting themselves and are gradually sinking into darkness. How do they imagine they will be able to progress and perfect themselves as long as they do not know, or refuse to admit, the existence above them of this sublime hierarchy of angels, archangels, etc., all the way up to the Lord? Because they cut themselves off from the ascending chain of beings, they have nothing and nobody with which to connect, to supply them with energies of a higher order, and help them progress along the road of evolution. Of course they are able to live, to manage materially, but from the spiritual point of view they stagnate, they gradually become mortified. Whereas those who are conscious of the existence of spiritual hierarchies always see this light before them and are given the impetus to progress.

How did the masculine principle – 1, create the feminine principle – 0 – matter? By bending back and joining together its two extremities. At that moment the circle is formed, and the circle represents matter, the universe as a whole. 1 – the creative principle, therefore comes first in all things, and 0 – creation, or what is created, must follow. By putting 1 before 0 we increase its power 10 times: 1 becomes 10. If, on the other hand, we do the opposite – 01, we reduce its strength and its value 10 times.

Let us now translate this to the inner life. If you put yourself, that which has been created – in other words 0, first, and 1 – the divine principle, in second place, behind you, then you reduce your qualities and your ability to progress. Whereas if you say: 'Lord, only You are truly great, powerful and wise, I shall always put You before me in first place and I shall follow You,' you increase your capabilities: you become 10. That is the attitude of truly spiritual people: they put the Lord first, so they receive good advice, and they are well guided.

When a child learns to read it starts by identifying the letters of the alphabet. Once it has learnt them well, it can gradually identify them in the words it comes across, until the day it is able to read whole sentences. The same applies to the disciple who, during the course of his initiation, passes through numerous phases in the course of which he gradually begins to see and make out the letters of the great cosmic book, which are the basic elements of creation. And when John writes at the beginning of his Gospel: 'In the beginning the Word already was. The Word was in God's presence, and what God was, the Word was. …and through him all things came to be …' it means that in the beginning all the principles of the divine alphabet came into action: from top to bottom of creation, right to the physical plane, they reproduced the same structures they had created up above. Everything that exists on the physical plane can be considered as words, sentences, poems composed with different elements of the Word.

Do you believe that when people say 'I', they really know what they are talking about? When they say: 'I am … (unwell or in good health, unhappy or happy); I want … (money, a car, a wife); I have … (such and such a wish, taste, opinion),' they really believe they are talking about themselves. That is exactly where they are mistaken. Since they have never analyzed themselves in sufficient depth to know their true nature, they identify themselves incessantly with this 'I', which is represented by their physical body, their instincts, their desires, their feelings and their thoughts. However, if they seek to find their inner self through study and meditation, they will discover that, beyond the superficiality, this 'I' they are looking for is an integral part of God Himself. The truth is that there is no multitude of separate beings, only one single Being who works through all beings, moving them and manifesting within them, even if they are not aware of it. The day they come to feel this reality, people will come closer to the divine Source whence all have their origin.

When it is time to pray and meditate your mind is often elsewhere. And when you need to concentrate on your work you often say to yourself: 'Oh, I should be meditating. I should spend some time in prayer,' and there again you are not focused, so you do your work badly. Watch yourself and you will see how often your state of mind is not in harmony with what you are doing. When you are cooking, doing the washing-up or driving the car, that is not the time to say: 'Oh, I should do some meditation.' You should be focused on the present in everything you do, because there is a time and a place for everything. Otherwise you will find that there is time for nothing because your mind is never focused on the task in hand, and you are never, really, anywhere.

The issue of freedom is far from clear in people's minds. Those who believe that being free means to be dependent on nothing and no one do not realize the danger they are in; since their heads and souls are empty there are voids everywhere into which all that is negative and dark is ready to rush. They want to be free, yes, but in reality they end up being totally drowned by other forces they do not know. You see this all too often. The devil will find work for anyone whose mind is not filled with divine thought: he will coax this person into dangerous adventures and acts of extravagance and foolishness, which of course lead to the usual consequences. And this because they were 'free' – or so they thought.

We must be committed, filled, occupied, taken over by heaven. Only then are we shielded and truly free. Nothingness does not exist, which is why you must do everything in your power *not* to be freed from heaven and the light; you must put yourself at the disposal of the celestial forces in order to receive endless blessings. Human beings can find freedom only if they are committed, and submit themselves to heaven.

Once people put on the 'tinted spectacles' of a religion, a philosophy or a little group, they end up losing sight of everything else. What is the use of religion if it hides the splendour of what God has created and the possibility of returning to Him?

The Church has warped people to such an extent that it is now no longer possible to make them understand the marvels of creation. They can understand what they themselves have created, yes: but God's creation does not interest them much, and they consider it unworthy of their attention. Of course, should you ask them they would not say they feel superior to God, but in practice that is just what they are doing – putting themselves above Him. The clergy should say: 'My children, respect life, because everything is sacred, all created things are talismans placed everywhere by God. Thank Him for the light of the sun and the stars, for the air, the water, everything nature provides.' But instead, all that matters to them is their own little world – the Host, rosaries, medals – the rest of the universe does not matter. And that is how, in the end, the rites established by the Church end by obscuring true religion.

Because they themselves are dishonest, sly and malicious, many people cannot believe that there is such a thing as an honest, sincere and good person. Yes, they judge others according to their own natures and that is why they are always suspicious. Those, however, who are noble and unselfish find it difficult to see malice, betrayal, or treachery because they also see others according to their own qualities. People can only see through their own eyes, and what their eyes see is formed by their own thoughts, feelings, desires and inclinations. If you meet someone who talks only about another's faults, be aware that in fact these faults belong to the speaker himself: because if he were noble, good, honest, and had love, above all, he would also see those same qualities reflected in others.

As soon as you venture into the esoteric sciences you discover magic and, more particularly, black magic. You would do well to stay clear of it, however, and especially not allow yourself to be frightened of falling victim to black magic. If you start to believe you could be affected by black magic, you are already attracting negative energies. Indeed, the moment you become weak and vulnerable you attract bad energies and every obscure thing floating in the atmosphere. It is the same with epidemics: if you are weak and receptive, you will catch bugs from the people you meet, whereas if you are robust, resistant and emissive, you come through unscathed.

So do not worry about black magic. Strengthen yourself and think of the light, work with the light and it is this light within you which will repel all that is negative. A wheel turning fast throws off all dirt, but as soon as it starts to slow down all the dirt sticks. The spring that flows vigorously sweeps away the leaves and twigs which could block it. So, do not succumb to mental laziness: be like the fast flowing spring.

You should never forget that human beings are at the border of the higher and lower worlds. The Christian religion expresses this idea with the image of the guardian angel who stands on the right, and the devil who stands on the left. The angel advises and enlightens whilst the devil seeks to lead astray, and so make human beings his victim. This is a rather simplistic way of putting things, but that is how it is in reality. In fact human beings have two natures: a lower nature and a higher nature. Depending on their degree of evolution they favour one or the other, and that is how they come into contact with the spirits of darkness, or with the spirits of light. Some people say that they do not believe in the entities of the invisible world. Well, whether they believe in them or not is irrelevant: their lower nature and their higher nature are there and it is impossible not to see them. It is up to each one of us to decide which influence we will accept.

Watch what you say: do not engage in big talk, do not commit yourself lightly, because you will provoke the invisible world and you will then have great trouble in keeping your commitments. In fact, you will not succeed.

A man swears he will never get married. Some time later he meets a woman. This woman, who is in fact the least able to make him happy, makes him lose his head and he marries her. Why? Because there are entities in the invisible world who, seeing this man so sure of himself, want to put him to the test. They try him to see what he is capable of, and very soon he succumbs. That is how people often do exactly the opposite of what they so adamantly professed, or promised.

In some countries it is the custom for a person to touch wood when saying something. This may seem superstitious, but this gesture says a great deal. It shows that, whilst they are talking, people are conscious of provoking invisible entities, and they touch wood to ward off misfortune.

As human beings we are linked to beings above us – the angels, the archangels and God Himself, as well as to beings below us – animals, plants and minerals.

Let us take the example of the two currents circulating in the trunk of a tree. The ascending current takes raw sap to the leaves, where it is refined, whilst the descending current takes this processed sap to feed the tree. In the cosmic Tree man is placed so that these two currents pass through him, and he must learn to work consciously with them. When he has succeeded in attracting wisdom, light and love from heaven, he passes these qualities on to the beings below him and linked to him, right on down to the minerals. Then, thanks to another current, these forces ascend from the minerals to the upper realms of creation. He who consciously binds with this living chain of beings is immersed in joy, light and peace.

When you seek a companion with whom to set up a family you have to make an effort to come out of yourself, to be more attentive, more understanding and more generous. However, people make the mistake of failing to understand that they should widen this family circle and extend their love to other creatures and to the whole universe. That is why they are still not happy even though they may have a wife, children, a job and a country to which they belong: because they have not yet managed to widen the circle of their love. Happiness is loving endlessly, not limiting this love to one person, or two, ten or a hundred... Go on loving those you love, but also love the angels, the archangels, all the celestial hierarchies, the Lord; and in this way your family and friends will find themselves enriched, stronger, improved and purified by all the sublime states you are cherishing in your heart and in your soul. Widen the circle of your love so that you may encounter all the higher creatures, and you will receive inspiration, support and protection.

The symbolic path of the sublimation of the sexual force goes from Yesod, passing through Tiphareth, to Kether. The highest extremity of the central pillar, the holiness of Kether, the crowned head, has its origins in the purity of Yesod, the sexual organs. The holiness of Kether is the sexual energy which the disciple endeavours to sublimate, thanks to the powers of Tiphareth, until this force can manifest itself higher up, like a golden light above his head. And that is the aim of initiation: to be able to control a raw force which drags us downwards, make it change direction, and then work on this quintessence so as to transform it into an aura of light.

The sceptre and the globe are emblems of royalty and, more generally, of power. Each time someone is depicted holding a sceptre in the right hand and a globe in the left we know that the person must be royal. However, what do we know of the deep meaning of these two objects? And do monarchs themselves really know what these objects represent?

The sceptre is usually considered to be the symbol of authority, and the globe the symbol of the territory over which this authority reigns. In reality these symbols have an even deeper meaning. The sceptre and globe represent the two principles of masculine and feminine. The masculine principle is always represented by a straight line – a sceptre, a caduceus, a lance, a sword, a pillar, a tree, etc., and the right hand. The feminine principle is represented by a curved line – all hollow, rounded objects, a sphere, a vase, a dish, as well as a chasm, a cave, and the left hand. When a person holds the sceptre and the globe, this signifies that he understands the two principles and knows how to work with them.

Many people are moved by an ideal of justice, honesty or goodness, but they do not know how to act and, continually in conflict with others, they end up discouraged. So, what should they do? Change their methods. However noble your ideal may be, do not concern yourself with others, work only at perfecting yourself. That is how, very gradually, whenever you meet people, you will impress them with your light and, as they look at you, it will become all too clear to them that they are squelching around in mud. Whereas if you try to visit them in their own mud, you too will sink into it and will become as filthy as they are. Work only at becoming luminous and, even if you say nothing, whenever others see you they will understand it is they themselves who have gone astray.

A precious stone, however small, is a particle of matter able to contain a cosmic force within it. Do not take it for granted that it will protect you, cure you or give you powers, however: if you do no spiritual work, a precious stone will be of no use to you. A stone is like an antenna and, like an antenna you need to give it a task – messages to transmit. Behind this stone forces are circulating and vibrating, but it is up to you to give them direction. Every precious stone has already been prepared by nature to capture certain energies from the cosmos, and to diffuse them and propagate them. Simply possessing a precious stone is not enough to benefit from its virtues. You must learn to use it to work on your inner self.

Life is created through an oscillation between opposite forces or situations. This law applies to all fields. For instance, the abundance and variety of riches on the surface of our planet is due to the fact that this surface is not flat, with many different levels ranging from high summits to the depths of the sea and the earth. The diversity in climate, flora, fauna, etc., from which, to some extent, stems the diversity of civilizations, arises from the fact that the surface of the earth is not level, and that is wonderful.

Human beings should not be all on the same level either. Why? So there may be a great circulation of fruitful exchanges between them. The only thing they should have in common is a high ideal, the desire always to go forward in love and in the light. For the rest, let differences remain. It is those differences which make their lives so rich and beautiful.

Astrology usually only takes the chart of physical birth into account. That is not enough, however, because a person's destiny cannot be determined on the basis of these indications alone. The chart of conception must also be considered, as well as the chart of the second birth, which is the time when the illuminated, renewed person accedes to the divine world, when his consciousness becomes superconsciousness – the consciousness of Christ. It is preferable to choose a propitious celestial moment in which to conceive a child on earth, but it is not necessary to study astrology to determine the second birth. If people live according to the laws of love, wisdom and purity, that is enough to ensure they have a second birth, and enter the new life: the Kingdom of God.

December 27

Because Jesus said to his disciples in the Garden of Gethsemane: ' Stay awake, and pray ...' many Christians throughout history have taken this to be a directive for everyday life. So the poor creatures have woken themselves up in the middle of the night to say their prayers, fighting tiredness and disrupting their bodies' natural rhythms. We need sleep to allow our bodies to rest. It is not so much on the physical plane that we should stay awake – 'stay awake' is above all a precept for the spiritual plane. 'To be vigilant' means to connect through thought to the being within us who never sleeps. We need to join with this being. This eternal watcher dwells between our two eyebrows. He sees everything, he records everything, he understands everything. Only when we succeed in uniting with him can we properly comply with the precept of Jesus: 'Stay awake, and pray'.

The caduceus of Hermes is a representation of the structure of man: the two serpents entwined around the wand are the two negative and positive currents that wind around either side of the spine. The Hindus call them Ida and Pingala, and they call the central channel inside the spine Soushoumna. An initiate is a person who knows how to work with both currents. As his work progresses he acquires powers that allow him to act on nature, on himself and on others. That is why the caduceus has become the symbol of medicine. The caduceus of Hermes represents a whole philosophy and discipline of life. It teaches us how to work with the two negative and positive currents which circulate in the universe. A true initiate, who works with the two principles, who knows the power of the two principles as an instrument, a weapon, a medicine – this initiate possesses true powers.

All people are capable of becoming stronger and improving their health without outside help, but to achieve this they must learn to concentrate on what is alive within them. Yes, because only living elements can fight illness. Suppose you have an abscess or a wound: if the living entities of your organism capable of healing the wound, or removing the impurities from the abscess, are anaesthetized because of the chaotic life you lead, the abscess or wound will become inflamed. Then tetanus or gangrene will set in and the leg or arm will have to be amputated. You may well use all the disinfectants, ointments and dressings in existence, but if the living entities within you do not have the right conditions in which to work properly, all exterior remedies will be powerless. Whereas if your inner workers are allowed to work freely, even if there is nothing or no one to offer help from elsewhere, they will cure everything. So it is quite straightforward: you must change your attitude and put your spiritual life first if you want to strengthen the life within you.

The soul is hungry and the spirit is thirsty. The soul eats fire and the spirit drinks light. The spirit is a masculine principle, the soul a feminine principle, and they each feed themselves with the complementary element. The soul – which aspires to a positive, active and dynamic principle – eats fire, whereas the spirit – which is masculine – needs to feed on the feminine principle, and drink light.

Just as the masculine principle begets the feminine principle, fire begets light. Light is a manifestation, an emanation of fire. When you light a fire it produces light. And the purer the materials that feed this fire the more subtle and bright is the light.

Do you feel the harmony we create all together when we sing? Tomorrow a new year starts and tonight we can say we have been singing for the year which has passed. That year is very pleased because its departure is immersed in love. As for the new year, we can already start to prepare it consciously this evening by focusing on one point: a quality to be developed, a bad habit to fight, or a project to realize for the glory of God. By focusing on this thought, this wish, it is as if you are laying the foundation stone, and then all the luminous spirits of nature will come to your aid and help you accomplish your divine project. That is what you should be concentrating on at the end of the year. Unfortunately, not many people do. Most are getting ready to succumb to all kinds of excesses. Not surprising, therefore, that the year then turns out badly for them. So all you who are disciples of the divine school, endeavour to receive the new year within you by placing yourselves under the sign of light.

The three fundamental activities which characterize human beings are thinking (by means of the intellect or mind), feeling (by means of the heart), and doing (by means of the physical body). You must not believe that only the physical body is material; the heart and mind are also material instruments, but the matter of which they are made is far subtler than that of the physical body.

HIGHER NATURE

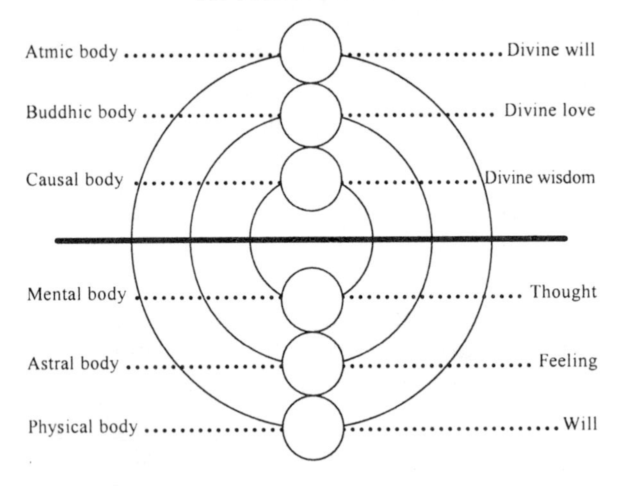

LOWER NATURE

An age-old esoteric tradition teaches that the support or vehicle of feeling is the astral body, and that of the intellect, the mental body. But this trinity, made up of our physical, astral, and mental bodies, constitutes our imperfect human nature, and the three faculties of thought, feeling, and action also exist on a higher level, their vehicles being respectively the causal, buddhic, and atmic bodies which go to make up our divine self.

In the diagram, the three large concentric circles indicate the relationship which links the lower and the higher bodies. The physical body, which represents strength, will, and power on the material level, is linked to the atmic body, which represents divine power, strength, and will. The astral body, which represents our egotistical, personal feelings and desires, is linked to the buddhic body, which represents divine love. The mental body, which represents our ordinary, self-serving thoughts, is linked to the causal body, which represents divine wisdom.

(*Man's Psychic Life: Elements and Structures*,
Izvor Collection No. 222, chap. 3.)

TREE OF LIFE

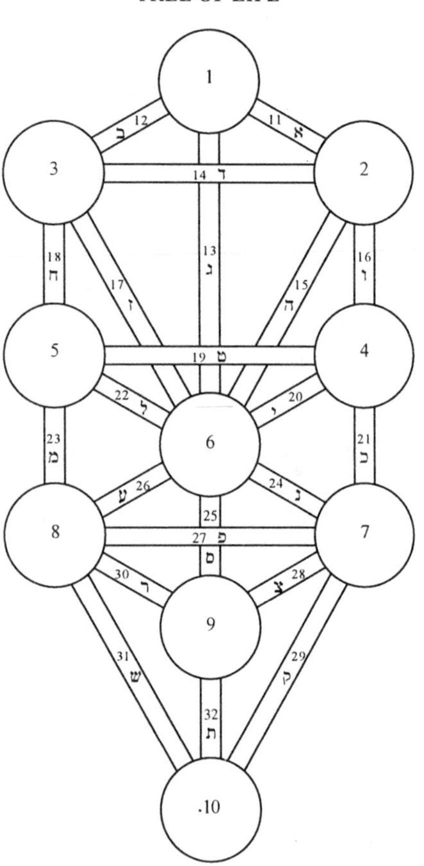

1
12 ב
11 א
3
14 ד
2
18 ח
17 ז
13 ג
15 ה
16 ו
5
19 ט
4
22 ל
20 י
6
23 מ
21 כ
26 ע
24 נ
8
25 ס
27 פ
7
30 ר
28 צ
9
31 ש
29 ק
32 ת
.10

TREE OF LIFE

1. Ehieh
Kether – *Crown*
Metatron
Hayot HaKadosh – *Seraphim*
Rashith HaGalgalim – *First Swirlings (Neptune)*
♆

3. Jehovah
Binah – *Understanding*
Tzaphkiel
Aralim – *Thrones*
Shabbathai – *Saturn*
♄

2. Yah
Chokmah – *Wisdom*
Raziel
Ophanim – *Cherubim*
Mazloth – *The Zodiac (Uranus)*
♅

5. Elohim Gibor
Geburah – *Severity*
Kamaël
Seraphim – *Powers*
Maadim– *Mars*
♂

4. El
Chesed – *Mercy*
Tzadkiel
Hashmalim – *Dominations*
Tzedek – *Jupiter*
♃

8. Elohim Tzebaoth
Hod – *Glory*
Raphaël
Bnei Elohim – *Archangels*
Kokab – *Mercury*
☿

7. Jehovah Tzebaoth
Netzach – *Victory*
Haniel
Elohim – *Principalities*
Noga –*Venus*
♀

9. Shadai El Hai
Yesod – *Foundation*
Gabriel
Kerubim – *Angels*
Levana – *Moon*
☽

6. Eloha vaDaath
Tiphareth – *Beauty*
Mikhaël
Malakhim – *Virtues*
Shemesh – *Sun*
☉

10. Adonai Melek
Malkuth – *The Kingdom*
Uriel (Sandalfon)
Ishim – *Beatified Souls*
Olem HaYesodoth – *Earth*

There are five aspects to be studied in each Sephirah:

- *the name of God*
- *the name of the Sephirah*
- *the leader of the angelic order*
- *the angelic order*
- *the name of the planet*

The Tree of Life is a symbolic figure which contains in condensed form the whole of initiatic science, the teachings of all initiates. It can be compared to a grain or seed; plant it and from it will spring the portrait of creation and all created beings. This figure can be an extremely important pantacle, one of the most powerful instruments of magic that it is possible to have. It contains everything: all the principles, all the elements, all the factors with which God created the world.

In the Tree of Life you have a system which can help you to avoid dispersing the efforts you devote to your spiritual work. If you work constantly with this figure for years, you will find that it brings order and balance to your life; everything within you will become organized and harmonious. Every time you have a moment to spare you can call to mind the Tree of Life and, by focusing on one Sephirah, strive to develop the qualities or energies it contains. Whatever you stand most in need of, be it light or love, strength, protection, generosity, justice, or life, look for it in the Tree of Life. The Tree of Life is there for us, for the sons and daughters of God who need to be nourished by divine life.

Omraam Mikhaël Aïvanhov

(*The Fruits of the Tree of Life*,
Complete Works, vol. 32, chap. 3)

By the same author:

(Translated from the French)

Izvor Collection

201 – Toward a Solar Civilization
202 – Man, Master of his Destiny
203 – Education Begins Before Birth
204 – The Yoga of Nutrition
205 – Sexual Force or the Winged Dragon
206 – A Philosophy of Universality
207 – What is a Spiritual Master?
208 – The Egregor of the Dove or the Reign of Peace
209 – Christmas and Easter in the Initiatic Tradition
210 – The Tree of the Knowledge of Good and Evil
211 – Freedom, the Spirit Triumphant
212 – Light is a Living Spirit
213 – Man's Two Natures: Human and Divine
214 – Hope for the World: Spiritual Galvanoplasty
215 – The True Meaning of Christ's Teaching
216 – The Living Book of Nature
217 – New Light on the Gospels
218 – The Symbolic Language of Geometrical Figures
219 – Man's Subtle Bodies and Centres
220 – The Zodiac, Key to Man and to the Universe
221 – True Alchemy or the Quest for Perfection
222 – Man's Psychic Life: Elements and Structures
223 – Creation: Artistic and Spiritual
224 – The Powers of Thought
225 – Harmony and Health
226 – The Book of Divine Magic
227 – Golden Rules for Everyday Life
228 – Looking into the Invisible
229 – The Path of Silence
230 – The Book of Revelations: a Commentary
231 – The Seeds of Happiness
232 – The Mysteries of Fire and Water
233 – Youth: Creators of the Future
234 – Truth, Fruit of Wisdom and Love
235 – 'In Spirit and in Truth'
236 – Angels and other Mysteries of The Tree of Life
237 – Cosmic Balance, The Secret of Polarity

Books by Omraam Mikhaël Aïvanhov
(translated from the French)

Complete Works

Volume 1 – The Second Birth
Volume 2 – Spiritual Alchemy
Volume 5 – Life Force
Volume 6 – Harmony
Volume 7 – The Mysteries of Yesod
Volume 10 – The Splendour of Tiphareth
The Yoga of the Sun
Volume 11 – The Key to the Problems of Existence
Volume 12 – Cosmic Moral Laws
Volume 13 – A New Earth
Methods, Exercises, Formulas, Prayers
Volume 14 – Love and Sexuality (Part I)
Volume 15 – Love and Sexuality (Part II)
Volume 17 – 'Know Thyself' Jnana Yoga (Part I)
Volume 18 – 'Know Thyself' Jnana Yoga (Part II)
Volume 25 – A New Dawn:
Society and Politics in the Light of Initiatic Science (Part I)
Volume 26 – A New Dawn:
Society and Politics in the Light of Initiatic Science (Part II)
Volume 29 – On the Art of Teaching (Part III)
Volume 30 – Life and Work in an Initiatic School
Training for the Divine
Volume 32 – The Fruits of the Tree of Life
The Cabbalistic Tradition

Brochures:
New Presentation

301 – The New Year
302 – Meditation
303 – Respiration
304 – Death and the Life Beyond

Daily Meditations:
A thought for each day of the year

Audio-cassettes:
KC2510A – The Laws of Reincarnation (2 cassettes)

Editor-Distributor

Editions PROSVETA S.A. - B.P. 12 - 83601 Fréjus Cedex (France)

Tel. 04 94 40 82 41 - Télécopie 04 94 40 80 05 - E-Mail: international@prosveta.com

Distributors

AUSTRALIA
QUEST, 484 Kent Street
2000 Sydney

AUSTRIA
HARMONIEQUELL VERSAND
A- 5302 Henndorf Hof 37
Tel and fax (43) 6214 7413

BELGIUM
PROSVETA BENELUX
Liersesteenweg 154 B-2547 Lint
Tel (32) 3/455 41 75 Fax 3/454 24 25
N.V. MAKLU Somersstraat 13-15
B-2000 Antwerpen
Tel. (32) 34 55 41 75
VANDER S.A.
Av. des Volontaires 321
B-1150 Bruxelles
Tel. (32) 27 62 98 04 Fax 27 62 06 62

BRAZIL
NOBEL SA – Rua da Balsa, 559
CEP 02910 - São Paulo, SP

BULGARIA
SVETOGLED
Bd Saborny 16 A appt 11 – 9000 Varna

CANADA
PROSVETA Inc. – 3950, Albert Mines
North Hatley (Qc), J0B 2C0
Tel. (819) 564-3287 Fax. (819) 564-1823
in Canada, call toll free: 1-800-584-8212
e-mail: prosveta@prosveta-canada.com

COLUMBIA
PROSVETA
Avenida 46 n° 19 - 14 (Palermo)
Santafe de Bogotá
Tel. (57) 232-01-36 – Fax (57) 633-58-03

CYPRUS
THE SOLAR CIVILISATION BOOKSHOP
73 D Kallipoleos Avenue - Lycavitos
P. O. Box 4947, 1355 – Nicosia
Tel: 02 377503 and 09 680854

GERMANY
PROSVETA Deutschland
Postfach 16 52 – 78616 Rottweil
Tel. 0741-46551 – Fax. 0741-46552
eMail: Prosveta.de@t-online.de
EDIS GmbH, Daimlerstr 5
82054 Sauerlach
Tel. (49) 8104-6677-0
Fax. (49) 8104-6677-99

GREAT BRITAIN
PROSVETA
The Doves Nest, Duddleswell Uckfield,
East Sussex TN 22 3JJ
Tel. (01825) 712988 - Fax (01825) 713386
E-Mail: prosveta@pavilion.co.uk

GREECE
EDITIONS PROSVETA – J. VAMVACAS
Montsopoulou 103 - 18541 Le Pirée

HOLLAND
STICHTING PROSVETA NEDERLAND
Zeestraat 50
2042 LC Zandvoort

HONG KONG
SWINDON BOOK CO LTD.
246 Deck 2, Ocean Terminal
Harbour City – Tsimshatsui, Kowloon

IRELAND
PROSVETA
The Doves Nest
Duddleswell Uckfield,
East Sussex TN 22 3JJ, U.K.

ITALY
PROSVETA Coop.
Casella Postale
06060 Moiano (PG)

LUXEMBOURG
PROSVETA BENELUX
Liersesteenweg 154 B-2547 Lint

NORWAY
PROSVETA NORDEN
Postboks 5101 – 1501 Moss

NEW ZEALAND
PSYCHIC BOOKS
p.o. Box 87-151
Meadowbank, Auckland 5

PORTUGAL
PUBLICAÇÕES
EUROPA-AMERICA Ltd
Est Lisboa-Sintra KM 14
2726 Mem Martins Codex

ROMANIA
ANTAR
Str. N. Constantinescu 10
Bloc 16A - sc A - Apt. 9
Sector 1 - 71253 Bucarest

SPAIN
ASOCIACIÓN PROSVETA ESPAÑOLA
C/ Ausias March n° 23 Ático
SP-08010 Barcelona
Tel (34) (3) 412 31 85 - Fax (3) 302 13 72

SWITZERLAND
PROSVETA
Société Coopérative
CH - 1808 Les Monts-de-Corsier
Tel. (41) 21 921 92 18
Fax. (41) 21 922 92 04
e-Mail: prosveta@swissonline.ch

UNITED STATES
PROSVETA U.S.A.
P.O. Box 49614
Los Angeles, California 90049
Tel and Fax (310) 458 3331

VENEZUELA
J. L. Carvajal
Apartado postal - Puerto Ordaz - 1038
Estado Bolivar

PRINTED IN FRANCE IN SEPTEMBER 1998
EDITIONS PROSVETA, Z.I. DU CAPITOU
B.P.12 – 83601 FRÉJUS
FRANCE

– N° d'impression: 2506 –
Dépôt légal: Septembre 1998
Printed in France